To Ken

ERNIE HARWELL
LIFE AFTER BASEBALL

Ernie Harwell

Credits

Editor: Maureen Ground
Designer: Chris Clonts
Copy editing: Tim Marcinkoski, Shelly Solon, Terrance Collins, Bill Collison and the Free Press sports copy desk.
Photo editor: Diane Weiss
Cover photo: Kirthmon F. Dozier
Back cover photo: Chip Somodevilla
Photo assistants: Naheed Choudhry, Kara Fulgenzi, Rose Ann McKean, Jessica Trevino, Kathryn Trudeau
Sports editor: Gene Myers
Design and graphics director: Steve Dorsey
Project coordinator: Dave Robinson
Special thanks: Laurie Delves

Detroit Free Press

600 W. Fort St.
Detroit, Mich. 48226
www.freep.com

Other recent books by the Free Press:

Life Lessons	Portraits of War	Razor Sharp: Drew Sharp
Stories From	Hockey Gods	Motoons: Mike Thompson
My Life In Baseball	Hang 10	The Corner
Time Frames	The Detroit Almanac	Fishing Michigan

To order any of these titles, please call 800-245-5082 or go to www.freep.com/bookstore

To subscribe to the Free Press call 800-395-3300.

Other books by Ernie Harwell:

Stories From My Life In Baseball	Tuned to Baseball
The Babe Signed My Shoe	Diamond Gems

Ernie Harwell | Life After Baseball
ISBN 0-937247-45-6
$14.95

Dedication

To Mike Ilitch and family with deep appreciation for your loyalty ... especially my Comerica Park statue.

Table of Contents

*Thanks to the Free Press and all the people
who worked on the book.*

– Ernie Harwell

Introduction

"We interrupt this marriage for the base-ball season." That was the sign on our wall at home. And in a facetious way it described my summers for 55 years. But times have changed in the Harwell household, and this past year proved to my wife, Lulu, and me that there is life after baseball.

The difference began in spring training. We still went to Lakeland, Fla., and hung around with the Tigers. But no longer did I broadcast those spring games. I didn't have to worry about identifying No. 87 who just came over from Tigertown to get into the lineup in the eighth inning. And I didn't have to take those tedious auto trips to Ft. Myers or Port St. Lucie. Still, I mingled with players and fans and enjoyed my long-standing Florida friends.

The year passed with the speed of a Randy Johnson fastball. My life without baseball became a series of parades, walks and speeches. It seemed that if a guy burped in the movie theater, I'd get up and make a speech. I continued to write my column for the Free Press, telecast 27 vignettes for Fox Sports Net and write introductions for books.

The highlight of my year was my new Blue Cross/Blue Shield contract. The concept of this relationship started on Ernie Harwell Day, Sept. 15, 2002. My longtime friend and advisor, Gary Spicer, and Rick Cole, vice president of Blue Cross, were seated on the field during the ceremonies. They began to discuss the possibility of a long-term relationship between Blue Cross and me. Their informal chat culminated in a 10-year contract, with an option for another 10 years. This gives me incentive to live another 20 years, serving as a health advocate for this great organization.

I didn't stay completely away from the game I love – baseball. Fox Sports Net asked me to work with Mario Impemba, subbing for Rod Allen on the telecast of Roger Clemens' attempt to get his 300th career victory. The Rocket failed that afternoon, but the Yankees beat the Tigers in 17 innings.

I was the luncheon speaker at the Triple-A All-Star Game in Memphis and appeared that evening on an ESPN telecast with Bob Carpenter and Buck Martinez. I worked again with Buck when he and Chris Berman honored me as their guest announcer on the ESPN Legends series. We telecast the Texas-Yankees game at Yankee Stadium. That same week I was on radio and TV for the Brockton (Mass.) team. Later, the Brooklyn Cyclones commemorated my major league broadcast debut in 1948 with an invitation to work the Cyclone game at Coney Island with longtime friend Warner Fusselle. I also visited the former site of Ebbets Field to film vignettes about the old ballpark.

There was another broadcast when I returned home – at Greenfield Village – where I announced a delightful game in which players re-created baseball of the 1850s.

During the season I also worked with the Tigers organization, visiting suites at various games. I posed for photos, signed baseballs and enjoyed the company of the loyal suite-holders.

There were speeches, too. I traveled all over Michigan, learning about many great charities. I met wonderful, dedicated people. The liveliest, most exciting crowd all year was the high-octane Palace gathering at Jim Rome's 31st world tour stop.

There was great excitement at the 2002 Thanksgiving Parade. It was an honor to be grand marshal of that one. I led parades in Lansing and Frankenmuth, appreciating the civic pride and hard work that go into those events.

Two special guys highlighted my year as I pitched in to salute Detroit stalwarts Joe Falls of the Detroit News and weatherman Sonny Eliot. It was a tribute dinner for Joe and a roast for Sonny. All of us tried to let those guys know how much they meant to us and to our city.

There were so many exciting happenings during that first year of my life after baseball. Here are a few more I deposited into my memory bank: Speaking at the Marines' birthday bash and the Sigma Alpha Epsilon fraternity's Christmas celebration. ... Induction in Chicago to the Pitch and Hit Hall of Fame. ... The Bud Selig Award at my favorite hotel, the Pfister in Milwaukee.

My trip to Washington for a George Washington University-Smithsonian Institution presentation at the CNN studios. ... Emceeing the Michigan Sports Hall of Fame induction and waiting for the invisible Barry Sanders. Refusing, with deep appreciation, offers to be honored by the Cubs and Giants organizations at their stadiums. ... Accepting the Lou Gehrig Iron Man Award in Detroit and the Emory University Award at my alma mater. ... Joining

Scotty Bowman, Joe Schmidt and Chuck Daly for honors at the annual CATCH banquet. ... The Michigan Legislature saluting the '68 Tigers. ... A delightful Sunday dinner in New York with my friend Spicer, and Don and Becky Baylor. ... Praying for Don in his courageous battle with cancer. ... Getting back into songwriting with Brian Alexander and Dan Yessian. ... So many rewarding experiences. So many wonderful people.

I miss being around the Tigers and the other big leaguers.

But I didn't miss 4 a.m. arrivals in the next city, rain delays and being away from my family.

Yes, I'm still busy, and life after baseball is certainly worthwhile.

ERNIE HARWELL
Spring 2004

Talkin' Baseball

I've heard them all, and Scully is the best

Since listening to the 1926 World Series on the radio, I've made a lifetime study of baseball broadcasters. I've heard them all — good or bad. Even tried some broadcasting myself. All of which gives me a right to select the best of all time. My choice is Vin Scully.

As the Dodgers' announcer since 1950, Scully has set a record for longevity with the same team. He's in his 54th season. Like no other, he has developed baseball broadcasting into an art form. Vin is better than any other broadcaster, including Red Barber, Mel Allen or Bob Elson. To fans in southern California, Scully is Mr. Baseball — even more popular than the players. In a 1976 poll, Dodgers fans chose him as the most memorable personality. He outranked Sandy Koufax, Don Drysdale and all the other superstar players.

I had a minor role in Scully's ascent to fame. Two times in his career, he was my replacement. The first time came during the football season of 1949. Earlier that summer, Scully, just out of Fordham University, had worked at WTOP in Washington as a substitute announcer. On a trip to CBS in New York, he interviewed with Barber, the sports director and famous Brooklyn broadcaster.

I was broadcasting football that year on the CBS "College Football Roundup." Red had assigned me to the Maryland-Boston University game at Fenway Park. But when Warren Brown was unable to do the headline game of the "Roundup" — North Carolina vs. Notre Dame at Yankee Stadium — I was transferred to that game. To replace me, Barber called on Scully, who impressed everybody with his performance.

A few weeks later, Scully replaced me again. This time it was baseball — not football. After my second year with the Dodgers, the Giants came after me. I accepted their attractive offer and joined Russ Hodges as an announcer for the New Yorkers. Again, Barber called on Scully. Remembering Scully's success on the football broadcast, Barber hired him to replace me in the Dodgers' booth. Scully debuted in the spring of 1950 and has been with the Dodgers ever since.

He has carved out a magnificent career. I have heard them all, and there is no doubt in my mind that Vin Scully is the best.

Originally printed on June 11, 2003.

That ball was caught by a fan from ...

I always enjoy hearing reactions to our Tigers broadcasts. Jim Price, Dan Dickerson and I do the best we can. We please some folks and don't please others. That's to be expected.

It's amazing that more listeners respond to non-play-by-play comments than game descriptions. For instance, I receive all kinds of remarks about: "That ball was caught by a man (or lady) from ———."

"I was always baffled by that," some fans tell me. Others might say, "I was 16 years old before I figured out what you were doing."

Some listeners have speculated that I have seating charts to find out about hometowns. Others suggested I check with turnstile men for information. Now that the computer age has arrived, some suggest I use my PC for the desired town locations.

Most folks have figured me out by now. After all, I've been using this gimmick since the early 1960s. I never mentioned hometowns when I broadcast for the Dodgers, the Giants or the Orioles. I started after I came to Detroit — 13 or 14 years into my broadcasting career.

The custom started strictly by accident. A batter hit a foul into the stands. On the spur of the moment I said, "That foul was caught by a man from Saginaw (or some other place)." A few days later I did it again. I began to say it often.

After a while people would stop me when I walked through Tiger Stadium. "Hey, let a guy from

Windsor catch one tonight," a fan might say. Or some lady would say, "I'm from Battle Creek. Can't somebody from our town catch a foul ball?"

During question-and-answer sessions at banquets, I'd always get one or two questions about the hometown gimmick. "How do you know where those people are from who catch foul balls?" was the most popular query. So, I finally came up with an answer.

Here's my answer: I can best respond by relating a story that happened to Casey Stengel when he was managing the Mets. A tall, gangly young man approached Casey during spring training.

"Mr. Stengel," he said. "I'm good enough to pitch in the big leagues, and I'd like to pitch for you."

"Is that right?" Casey said. "What are your credentials?"

"Well, in college I pitched and played outfield. Last year, I hit 35 home runs and had 120 RBIs in 90 games. I pitched two no-hitters and once struck out 22 batters in one game. I stole 30 bases and never made an error. I'm fast, too. I can run the 100 meters in 9.9."

"That's impressive, son," Stengel told him. "Don't you have any weakness?"

The youngster lowered his eyes and looked at his shoes.

"Well," he said. "I do lie a little."

Originally printed on August 28, 2002.

Everyone makes mistakes, even broadcasters

In criminal lore, the police sometimes get the wrong man.

It happens in baseball broadcasting, too. Several weeks ago, Pittsburgh Pirates announcer Lanny Frattare broke into game coverage with the announcement that famous actor James Earl Jones had died.

Frattare had misunderstood a producer who had relayed him the news of the death of James Earl Ray, the convicted killer of Martin Luther King Jr.

Frattare corrected the mistake shortly after he had made it on his Pirates-Giants broadcast. During his errant report, Frattare had waxed nostalgically about Jones' role in the movie "Field of Dreams."

"A lot of us in the baseball world have good feelings about 'Field of Dreams' and the soliloquy Jones gave in it," Lanny said.

Later, he said: "I don't feel good about my booboo. In fact, I feel like a fool."

Join the club, Lanny. I've made many mistakes in my career and have often felt like a fool. It's an embarrassment, but it happens to all of us.

Gene Kelly, a fine announcer for the Philadelphia Phillies in the 1950s, suffered the same kind of chagrin.

Just before a night game at Shibe Park in Philadelphia, somebody told Kelly that Joe McCarthy had died. Moments later, Kelly went on the air with a moving tribute to the longtime major league manager. He recalled that McCarthy had never played in the major leagues but had led the Cubs to a pennant in 1929, then switched to the Yankees and won eight pennants for them. He related how "Marse Joe" had managed the Red Sox his final three seasons, coming close but never winning for Boston.

It was a long and flowery discourse. After Kelly had proceeded through five minutes of accolades for McCarthy, he took a commercial break. The phone in the booth rang.

"Gene," said a voice from the downtown studio. "That was a great tribute, but you had the wrong McCarthy. The one who died was Sen. Joe McCarthy."

Originally printed on May 19, 1998.

Knowing the score is most important

What's the score?"
"6-2."
"Who's winning?"
"The team with the six."

OK, so it's an old baseball joke. But it does point out a basic of play-by-play broadcasting. Everybody needs to know the score. It is the most important fact we can hear. My example is certainly not the best way to impart the score. Yet, too often, I hear announcers say, "It's a 6-2 game." Or: "That run cuts the Red Sox's lead to one." Or: "Now it's a one-run game."

The simplest, most effective way is to say, "The score is Yankees 6, Red Sox 2." That takes no longer and gives the listener the update.

Of course, it's imperative to give the score more often on radio than on television. TV displays the score on the screen. Still, many blind people follow the game on TV, and even sighted fans are sometimes away from the pictures but can still hear the sound.

I have heard radio and TV announcers switch to a commercial after an inning and not give the score. Coming back after the break, they often forget to give it. That is probably the most important time to hear the score. The announcer has been away for two minutes, and many fans have joined the broadcast.

No matter how many times you announce the

score, you can't give it too much. Fans don't pay close attention. Even if you announce the score, they miss it.

Also, they are going to the bathroom, getting in and out of their cars, and often reading or talking. So the score is a must.

The Tigers' announcers on radio and TV are better than most about giving the score. The late Red Barber, play-by-play's best technician, used an egg timer to remind himself about the need to do it often. But he used a three-minute timer, and I think that's too much time without a score.

In 55 years of major league broadcasting, I received one letter of complaint about giving the score too often. It was such a rare event that after I phoned the writer and talked with him, I saved the letter. The writer was Thad Bykowski of Bay City. On July 18, 1997, he wrote me a pleasant, well-phrased letter, and I appreciated his comments.

"Why," he asked, "do you insist on giving the score of the game 75 to 100 times during nine innings? You actually insult the listener by repeating the score so many times."

When I talked with Mr. Bykowski, I tried to explain my stance, using the same points I've used here. He was quite understanding. And I still think it's the best way to broadcast. Give the score. You can't do it too often.

Originally printed on May 10, 2003.

Stadium announcers have a colorful history

P ublic address announcers should be heard, not seen. The good ones are like good drivers and umpires. If they do their jobs correctly, they go practically unnoticed.

Dan York, who plies his trade at Comerica Park, is excellent. With a strong, clear, authoritative voice, he doesn't call attention to himself or interfere with the flow of the game. He is one of my favorites.

Before electronics, the PA men used megaphones — large cone-shaped devices — to amplify their voices. They made few announcements, usually only for the batteries and lineup changes.

One of my boyhood heroes was the PA man at Cleveland, Tom Manning. Manning got his job in a strange way. He was a newsboy. In those days, youngsters sold papers on the street. To grab attention and make a sale, they would shout out the headlines. Manning had such a strong voice he was voted "The Loudest Mouth in Cleveland."

A redhead with a sparkling personality, Manning graduated from his PA job into radio. It was Tom who broadcast the famous called-shot home run by Babe Ruth in the 1932 World Series.

When I worked in Brooklyn, I knew another colorful PA man — Tex Rickard. Tex had the same name as the famous boxing promoter of the 1920s, but there was no relation between the two. Even on the hottest afternoon at Ebbets Field, Tex wore a heavy, white wool sweater with "Dodgers" emblazoned across the front.

When a Dodger hit a home run, Rickard would greet him at home plate with a handshake — which put him in many photos on the back pages of the New York tabloids.

In the late '40s, Jimmy Powers, sports editor of the Daily News, was campaigning for more information for fans at the ballparks. "The patron who pays to see the game should be told at least as much as the radio listeners," he wrote.

The day after Powers' column appeared, the Cardinals jumped on Dodgers pitcher Preacher Roe in the first inning and raked him for six or seven runs before manager Burt Shotton could get to his bullpen. As Roe trudged off the mound with his head down, Rickard intoned, "Preacher Roe has left the game because he don't feel good."

Tex gave us another gem when he said, "Attention, please! Will the fans along the leftfield railing please remove their clothing."

Originally printed on April 26, 2003.

This writer made turns for the verse

All of us who talk or write sometimes make a wrong turn on a phrase. We might even be guilty of a malapropism and give a reader or listener a chuckle or two. Always, those malapropisms bring us good-natured ridicule.

Two long-standing baseball announcers who have made careers out of malapropisms are Ralph Kiner of the Mets and Jerry Coleman, voice of the Padres. Mistakes certainly have not diminished their careers. Kiner has been broadcasting for the Mets since their first season in 1962, and Coleman this year enters his 23rd year of airing Padres games.

But did you ever hear of Charles Wicker? Probably not. Wicker was a sports announcer and writer. He died several years ago, but for more than 30 years had been regarded as the king of fractured phrases.

As an announcer, he contributed, "And he slides into second with a stand-up double." On another broadcast, he yelled: "Here's the pitch. There's a long drive to deep, deep centerfield. The centerfielder goes back, back, back, but the ball curves foul."

Yet, it was as a writer for the New Orleans Times-Picayune that he reached his zenith. His lead on a high school football game went this way: "Holy Cross and Jesuit played to a 6-6 tie yesterday, but the game was much closer than the score would indicate."

During another high school game, a student was injured in a 30-foot fall from the top row of the stadium. The last paragraph of Wicker's story read: "The accident occurred when the victim leaned against 32 feet of railing which was missing."

When Charles turned his talents toward baseball, the results were just as amazing. He reported that a local schoolboy pitcher had given up only "one scattered hit."

Another Wicker classic was a reference to a high school pitcher who had been hit in the mouth by a line drive. The youngster's teeth had been replaced by a partial denture. Charles wrote: "Pitching for the Eagles will be Jack Flynn, who had his front teeth knocked out and replaced by a line drive."

Wicker's idea of transportation was different from other folks'. He once wrote: "The New Orleans Babe Ruth League champions will fly to the Southwest Regionals in Albuquerque, N.M., on an air-conditioned Greyhound bus."

When he was only 49 years old, Wicker was slowed by a serious heart attack. He retired from the newspaper business and founded an exclusive private school in suburban New Orleans. The school was named the N. Charles Wicker Academy.

A young lady who taught at that school was asked what the founder did there. "He doesn't teach English, does he?" she was asked.

"Oh, no," she answered. "Mr. Wicker doesn't teach English. He just services our candy machines."

All of us have a little Charles Wicker in us. We make our mistakes, and we have our lapses. We just don't happen to do it with as much color and verve as Wicker.

Originally printed on June 30, 1995.

Even after 50 years, friends are forever

Is there any greater thrill than seeing an old friend? How about seeing an old friend for the first time? That's what happened to me last fall.

I was making a speech at the Baseball Hall of Fame in Cooperstown, N.Y., in late October. As I entered the auditorium and started for the podium, I heard a voice say, "Hi, Ernie, I'm Jocko Maxwell."

"Jocko," I shouted. "I haven't heard from you in over 50 years. It's great to see you."

He was an old friend, but actually, I had never seen Jocko. But that's quite a story.

I had started my radio career with a nightly sports show on powerful, 50,000-watt WSB in Atlanta in late May 1940. A week after my first show, I received a letter from New York. Jocko Maxwell was the writer. He liked my show and wrote some nice comments about it. He told me he was a sportscaster in New York and also wrote a column for a Long Island paper. I was thrilled and flattered by my first so-called fan letter. I wrote back to thank him for the letter and we began to correspond.

I never met Jocko. But we kept exchanging letters. About the second year of our exchanges he enclosed a photograph of himself.

"Is my face red?" he wrote. "No. It's black. I bet you didn't know. Did you?"

No, I didn't know. It was a surprise to me that he was an African American. We continued to write each other while I spent four years in the Marines.

18

When I returned to civilian life in 1946, Jocko sent me a book he had written. It was an interesting view of the people in sports he had met and interviewed on his radio show.

After I went to Brooklyn to broadcast Dodgers games, I lost track of Jocko. I could not locate him. I don't remember why. But somehow we lost touch.

Imagine my surprise and thrill when he showed up at my speech in Cooperstown. He didn't come to the Hall of Fame to hear me. He was there on a trip with Christine V. Baird of the Newark Star-Ledger and her husband. Ms. Baird was writing a story about Jocko and his career.

Jocko, 93, was in a wheelchair. After my speech we had a long talk. He is sharp mentally, but can't move around too well. Otherwise, he seems healthy. He told me he was perhaps the first African American to have a sports radio show.

"I was broadcasting in Newark in 1929," he told me. "I still love sports — especially baseball."

Jocko makes his home in West Chester, Pa., and again — after more than 50 years — we are writing to each other.

Originally printed on August 21, 2002.

Heilmann played, talked good game

Sometimes the reader has a better idea for a column than the writer. Rod Gibson of Birmingham writes: "I have been a Tigers fan since before 1950. When I began listening, Harry Heilmann was the announcer. With all the hoopla about great Tigers — Cobb, Kaline, Greenberg, etc. — I never hear about Heilmann."

Gibson is right. This column is about Heilmann.

Before Ted Williams hit .406 in 1941, Heilmann was the last American Leaguer to do it — .403 in '23. Harry's lifetime average was .342, the same as Babe Ruth's. Next to Rogers Hornsby, Heilmann is regarded by many as the best right-handed hitter ever.

Imagine the money a hitter like that could command today. When Heilmann signed his first contract, he received only a spaghetti dinner.

After failing to make his high school team and flunking out of school, Harry worked as a bookkeeper for the Mutual Biscuit Co. of San Francisco in 1913. One day he bumped into Jim Riordan, manager of the Hanford semipro team. Riordan needed a third baseman. Although he never played the position, Heilmann agreed to give it a try. The pay was $10. Heilmann was the game's hero, doubling in two runs in the 11th inning to win it. A scout for Portland, Jim Richardson, saw the heroics and offered Heilmann a contract. Harry signed and that night received his bonus — a spaghetti dinner.

Heilmann played that 1913 season for Portland,

then in the Northwestern League. He batted .305 in 122 games. The league president was Fielder Jones, who also scouted for the Tigers. Jones suggested to Tigers owner Frank Navin that he draft Harry. Navin gave Heilmann a contract for $350 a month. In 1914, Harry played first base, second base and outfield, hitting .225.

When he received his contract the next spring for another $350, Heilmann balked. San Francisco had offered him $450 a month. The Tigers would not let Harry out of his contract, but they farmed him out to San Francisco, where he hit .364.

Heilmann returned to the majors in 1916. His Tigers career lasted through 1929. He played two years with the Reds before retiring to become an outstanding Tigers radio announcer.

In his Hall of Fame career, Heilmann won the batting title four times with averages of .394 (1921), .403 ('23), .393 ('25) and .398 ('27).

Heilmann never made a big salary, but was content with a good living, baseball fame and many loyal listeners and friends. Not bad for a guy whose signing bonus was a spaghetti dinner.

Originally printed on September 13, 2001.

Hall of fame broadcaster McDonald was a winner

The newest inductee into the broadcast wing of the Hall of Fame is Arch McDonald. With that name, McDonald would have been a natural spokesman for the famous hamburger chain. Think about it. First name, Arch. He was a big guy. Hence, Big Mac. And his last name was the name of the sponsor.

But Arch came too soon. His heyday was 1934-56, when he was the voice of the Washington Senators. Arch never broadcast for a winner. Washington had won the pennant in 1933, but none afterward.

McDonald began his radio career with the Senators' Class A Chattanooga (Tenn.) Lookouts. In Washington, he regaled his listeners with his Arkansas-tinged twang and his signature phrases. For Arch, runners were "ducks on the pond." When a Senator homered, McDonald would shout, "There she goes, Mrs. Murphy!" A pitch over the plate for Arch was "Right Down Broadway." But his most famous line was from his favorite song, "They Cut Down the Old Pine Tree." Arch employed that title phrase whenever a Senator made a dazzling play.

With the economy-minded Senators, McDonald doubled as Griffith Stadium's PA announcer. Once, before a game, he intoned, "Now, ladies and gentlemen, our national anthem." Then from the record player came "They Cut Down the Old Pine Tree."

After five years in Washington, Arch went to New York in 1939 to become the first voice of the Yankees.

He lasted less than a season. His down-home, easy style didn't fit New York's taste, so Arch came back to Washington for his final 17 years, and his young assistant, Mel Allen, took over the New York job.

McDonald put his inventive style on display when he recreated Senators road games from a drugstore window, three blocks from the White House.

Arch's career with the Senators ended in 1956 when the club made a sponsor change. He also broadcast Redskins football. After a football broadcast in New York, on Oct. 16, 1960, McDonald died of a heart attack on the train to Washington.

Originally printed on July 30, 1999.

If it was cliche, Richards could really turn on it

Like all of us, big league managers sprinkle their language with cliches. We've all heard them talk about "playing one game at a time" or "giving 110 percent."

Paul Richards, one of the most astute managers, used to sneer at these sayings. Besides being a master strategist, he was an intelligent student of the English language. As a one-time sports editor of the Waxahachie (Texas) Light, Richards could spot a cliche as easily as he could pick up a pitcher's mannerisms.

Richards once gave me his short list of time-frayed phrases from the mouths of his fellow managers and added a comment to each.

1. "I'd rather see him (the opposing batter) hit a home run than give him a walk." Comment: "This is not sensible at all. A walk surely won't hurt your team as much as a homer."

2. "Never throw a high curve." Comment: "All wrong again. Virgil Trucks, Ray Benge and Larry French are just a few of the outstanding pitchers who made a big league career throwing curves — and winning with them."

3. "I like speed." Comment: "I've never seen a manager yet who didn't."

4. "We ain't hitting." Comment: "This is supposed to excuse any defeat — even if it's an 11-8 beating."

5. "Don't walk him, but don't give him anything good to hit, either." Comment: "Wouldn't it be better if the manager simply told the pitcher to throw the ball?"

6. "Never throw a change-up with two strikes on the batter." Comment: "Why not? A change-up (a good one) is effective almost anytime, and sometimes with two strikes on the batter, it is more effective than ever because of the element of surprise."

7. "You're working too fast. Slow down. Or, you're working too slow. Throw the ball." Comment: "If the pitcher is getting batters out, it makes little difference how fast or how slow he is pitching. If he's not getting 'em out, it doesn't make any difference, either."

8. "Stick that slider somewhere you won't be using it. It's a bad pitch." Comment: "All wrong. The slider is one of the game's best pitches. It's one of the reasons today's pitchers are better than ever. And, more than any one factor, the slider is responsible for the current low batting averages."

Richards made these comments to me in the 1950s; most of them have stood the test of time. The possible exceptions might be his observations about pitchers being better than ever and current low batting averages.

Richards was manager of the Atlanta Crackers when I covered my first training camp in 1941. Richards also was the subject of the first article I wrote for a Detroit paper when, during World War II, he left his managing job with Atlanta to return to big league catching with the Tigers.

And he could spot a cliche better than most of us.

Originally printed on June 2, 1995.

Worst quotes turn out best

ecently on Channel 50, Al Kaline mentioned the unusual configuration of Fenway Park's rightfield corner. I tried to follow up by saying the corner does have some unusual nooks and crannies.

"Yes, Al," I said, "there are a lot of crooks and nannies out there." It was one more Harwellian slip to add to my always-growing list. But I'm not alone in this business. Let's look at some other crazy baseball quotes:

"I watch a lot of baseball on the radio." President Gerald Ford, 1978.

"Even Napoleon had his Watergate." Phillies manager Danny Ozark.

"Whenever the decision is made, I'll have the final hearsay." Tigers pitcher Mark Fidrych.

"He ain't no rocket surgeon." Unnamed Montreal Expo, evaluating a teammate.

"It's a beautiful day for a night game." Giants announcer Frankie Frisch.

"Too bad I wasn't a second baseman. Then I would have seen a lot more of my husband." Pete Rose's ex-wife, Karolyn.

"A lot of people my age are dead at the present time." Manager Casey Stengel.

"It could permanently hurt a batter for a long time." Pete Rose.

"He fakes a bluff." Announcer Ron Fairly.

"Pain don't hurt." Manager Sparky Anderson.

"The doctors x-rayed my head and found nothing."

Cardinals pitcher Dizzy Dean.

"Fans, don't fail to miss tomorrow's game." Announcer Dizzy Dean.

"His reputation preceded him before he got here." Yankees first baseman Don Mattingly.

Maybe these are crazy because English is such a crazy language. From the wisdom of the Internet, we get these examples:

There's no egg in eggplant nor ham in hamburger. There is neither apple nor pine in pineapple.

Quicksand can work slowly. Boxing rings are square. Writers write, but fingers don't fing, grocers don't groce, and hammers don't ham. People ship by truck and send cargo by ship. We have noses that run and feet that smell. We park on driveways and drive on parkways.

When stars are out, they are visible, but when lights are out, they are invisible.

A slim chance and a fat chance are the same. Yet, a wise man and a wise guy are opposites.

How can the weather be hot as hell one time, cold as hell the next?

No wonder baseball players and announcers say goofy things.

Originally printed on September 22, 1998.

More than a game

Lone seagull a sentry for dying trainer

When the lone seagull first appeared in front of their Jacobs Field dugout during a night game with the White Sox on July 15, the Cleveland Indians were in deep shock.

Their beloved trainer, Jimmy Warfield, was at the Cleveland Clinic in a coma and near death. Warfield was a close confidant of all the players. In 32 years as their trainer, his zest, intense passion for life and genuine warmth had touched all of them.

The Indians were accustomed to seagulls. Flocks often invaded Jacobs Field. The players had even recognized individual birds from time to time. But this one was different. And the Indians realized they had never seen this particular seagull before.

The bird was alone — not in the usual flock and not searching for food like the others. It was thin and scrawny. It even seemed scruffier and more weathered than the seagulls that frequented the ballpark.

With the game in progress, the gull walked near the corner of the Indians' dugout where Warfield and fellow trainer Paul Spicuzza always sat. The gull moved around the diamond, stopping near Jim Thome at first base and several times approaching pitcher C. C. Sabathia on the mound. White Sox batters had to shoo it away from the plate.

The next day the Indians visited Warfield at the Cleveland Clinic. After their sad good-byes, Jimmy died at 4:15 p.m. The ballclub had to make a decision. Should the game that night be played or postponed? The decision was to play.

The seagull appeared at batting practice that night. It landed in front of Warfield's dugout seat. It was not eating. It simply sat. Then it flew into the outfield and stayed around all night. It came back the next evening — again alone and not eating. It stationed itself behind shortstop Omar Vizquel and later moved toward first base and Thome.

The next game came the afternoon of July 18. The seagull was strangely absent — for the first time since Jimmy had been stricken.

The Indians conducted a memorial service that evening for Warfield in the Terrace Club at Jacobs Field. The seagull reappeared, walking around the field during the service. When the ceremony was over, teary-eyed players noticed the bird. They watched as it took flight and circled the bases. After completing its circuit it soared toward centerfield and disappeared into the night.

No one has seen the seagull since.

Originally printed on September 4, 2002.

Ichiro studies past, makes own history

Baseball's most fascinating player is Seattle's Ichiro Suzuki. Forget that he is a shoo-in for the American League rookie of the year award.

Or that he might be the league's MVP, lead the league in hitting or set a major league record with more than 257 hits for the season.

Instead, let's concentrate on other facets of his fascination.

He is the only player in baseball history known strictly by his first name. The back of his uniform reads "Ichiro." When Mariners manager Lou Piniella makes out his lineup, he writes in "Suzuki, Ichiro."

Our Japanese friends tell us there are more than two million Suzukis in their country, and the All-Star rightfielder deserves first-name recognition. His supporters revel in his international fame. Tracing Ichiro's ancestry to the 12th Century is another point of pride for the Suzukis.

Ichiro has a sense of history. Last winter, after he had agreed to come to America, he asked writer and television producer Brad Lefton to supply him with all kinds of information about our baseball heritage. He made a real effort to learn about our game.

Through the years, I've known many major leaguers. Most are much more interested in playing the game than knowing about its past. Some modern players know or care little about Lou Gehrig, Charlie

Gehringer or Walter Johnson. There are exceptions. Tony Clark is one. He has a special interest in Jackie Robinson's contribution to the game. Reggie Jackson was a tremendous fan — probably still is. Pete Rose was another who knew a great deal about the stars who had preceded him.

Isn't it ironic that a Japanese player — in his first year in America — is such a contrast to the American players in his attention to our history? Ichiro's interest in history extends to himself, too. He has a television crew taping his activities every day — for his own personal record. It's a sort of video diary of his first season in America.

When the season is over, Japanese television will use much of this material for a documentary about Ichiro. Such a program is sure to attract a huge audience. Ichiro enjoys the status of a rock star in his native land.

Interest there is so intense that the Japanese media following him this season had to be restricted to pool coverage of his activities. Before or after each game, the Japanese select one of their writers to represent all of them with questions for the man known by his first name.

Originally printed on September 9, 2001.

Little girl's ode to a dear, old friend

Perrie Marie Douglas of Forest, Ontario, was only 10 when she spoke in front of the entire St. John Fisher Elementary School. She was competing in a public speaker's contest, and her performance advanced her to the local Canadian Legion competition.

In my early school days I spoke and debated in contests. All my life I have made a study of public speaking. But at the age of 10, Perrie made one of the best declamations I have ever come across. Because of the speech's brilliance and the subject matter's appeal to me, I want you to read it.

"Last year I lost a very special friend. She was 80 years old. She wasn't related to me, but she was a very important part of my family. We loved to visit her even though she was almost two hours away.

"Mr. Mac and fellow students, I want to tell you about a grand old lady who played a big part in my life. She was born around the time that the Titanic sank. That was the start of a long and exciting existence. My great-great-uncle Nick knew her from the time they were both young. She was gray from the first time my grandfather met her. I don't remember the first time I met her because I was still a baby. It was always an exciting family event when we went to see her. My mother, my aunt and I went to see her several times a year.

"Visiting her wasn't at all like visiting others her age. She loved it when I danced and when I got loud.

34

I learned many new dances with her, like 'The Chicken Dance' and 'YMCA.' I remember once I yelled as loud as I could and she didn't even care. My friend always gave me my favorite food. She would feed you ice cream and popcorn and call it lunch.

"I really loved to visit her — she knew more about history than anyone else I know. Every time I visited her she had a different story to tell. The world around her changed a lot. In the 1920s she saw the beginning of motion pictures. She loved movies and eventually had the biggest screen she could get. The stock market crashed, and in the 1930s she saw the Great Depression hit. My friend was hurt by the lack of money around her, and she had fewer visitors because people couldn't afford to travel to see her.

"In the 1940s she saw her boys go off to war. Some joined the Army, some joined the Air Force, and the lucky ones in the Navy got to wear bell-bottoms. My friend saw big changes in the 1950s. People started having televisions in their homes. She saw rock 'n' roll music become popular. She herself loved music and had it playing whenever she had company. One of her best friends, Dan Grier, would often play the organ when he visited her, and there would be a great party with everybody singing and dancing.

"In the 1960s my friend saw hippies with their long hair, tie-dyed shirts, peace symbols and bell-bottoms. In the 1970s she heard disco music and she saw streakers. For some reason, those fools in the '70s thought it was a good idea to run naked through public events.

"In the 1980s my friend saw punk rockers and big hair. The 1980s were some of her best years, and not just because I was born in that decade. In the 1990s my friend saw people with their long hair, tie-dyed shirts, peace symbols and bell-bottoms . . . AGAIN!

"My friend was a little bit vain about her looks. Every year she would have a makeover, and she always got spruced up for visitors. She never looked finer than the last time I saw her. She was a real trendsetter — she even made people think that her quirks were quaint instead of silly.

"Over the span of her lifetime she met a lot of famous people, like Joe Louis, Aretha Franklin, Bob Seger, Steve Yzerman, Dale Jarrett, Derek Jeter and Big Bird. Once she introduced me to Darren McCarty from the Red Wings. She even made some television appearances.

"She had a special charm that no one could resist. I am sure going to miss that grand old lady, Tiger Stadium."

Originally printed on April 26, 2002.

Brash Eddie Stanky also had soft side

When Eddie Stanky died this week, I lost a true friend. With the New York Giants in the 1950s, we were always together — playing golf, fighting at cards, eating and riding trains together. Eddie was the fiercest competitor I ever knew. He was caustic and sarcastic — best with the needle since Betsy Ross.

To the public, he was a mean, hard-nosed competitor. Off the field, he was a true softie — putty in the hands of his wife, Dickie. His teammates gave him the utmost respect because they knew he would go the limit for them. When he played for the Brooklyn Dodgers, Branch Rickey said of him, "He can't run, he can't hit and he can't throw, but I'd rather have him on my team than any other player."

If you want to know what Stanky was really like, let me take you back to a golf game he and I had in the 1950s. It was just the two of us at the Bonnie Briar club in Larchmont, N.Y. The same caddie was carrying Eddie's bag and mine. On the first hole, Stanky started poorly. Already he had hit three shots. I had hit a long drive down the middle of the fairway. Stanky hooked a three-iron toward the woods and the out-of-bounds marker. The ball landed right on the boundary line. It was either out of bounds or barely in.

Eddie, the caddie and I walked over to take a look. Stanky stared at me. I said, "Ed, I don't know. It's so close. What do you think?"

37

"We'll ask the caddie," he said.

That was all right with me. I really wasn't being any great sport since it was almost certain I would win the hole with ease.

"Well?" Eddie asked the caddie. "Is it in or out of bounds?"

"Don't ask me, Mr. Stanky," the caddie replied. "A lady asked me for a ruling last week. I gave her one. She got mad, reported me to the pro, and I'm in trouble. I'm not making any ruling for you."

After that, the caddie started walking ahead of us, down the fairway toward my ball. I looked at Eddie. He was steaming. The veins on his neck were about to pop. He reached down, picked up his ball and threw it at our caddie. It whizzed past the caddie's ear and bounced down the fairway. Eddie cupped his hands to his mouth and yelled at the caddie, "You're gutless! I don't care what you call it, but call it something! Show me some courage!"

Now you know what my pal Eddie Stanky was really like.

Originally printed on June 11, 1999.

Remembering golf's Bob Jones

The Masters has become one of the great events in American sports. But I remember when it was little more that a fun gathering for a bunch of rich guys who loved golf.

Now, you might say the rich guys are the pro golfers and the famous tournament is more money than fun. When I broadcast the Masters in 1941, the winning purse was $1,500. This weekend the champion will take home $1 million.

The 1941 Masters was my first out-of-town broadcast. Still a rookie at WSB radio in Atlanta, I rode a bus to Augusta, where I stayed at the ancient Bon Air hotel. It was a gigantic wooden structure whose walls were about as thick as toilet paper. All the golf pros and other guests stayed there, and I was awed to mingle with the headliners. Plus, the hotel was on the American plan, meaning that meals were included in the cost of the room.

Young, healthy and with a great appetite, I took full advantage. It was the first time I had eaten steak for breakfast. Plus, I might be at a table with Sam Snead, Byron Nelson, Fred Astaire or Ty Cobb.

I didn't do play-by-play my first year. Instead, my job was to interview the golfers and give scores on my 6:15 p.m. broadcast. My first guest was the great Bob Jones. Jones was the real reason for the tournament. It attracted national coverage only because he played in it — his sole public appearance after his retirement.

Bob had agreed to let me interview him on top of the newly constructed tower behind the 18th green. In those days, nothing was recorded. If you did an interview, it had to be live. If the guest failed to show, too bad.

As Jones and I waited in the locker room for 6:15, a storm blew over Augusta. Violent rain swept the course. At 6:10 it was still raining hard. My interview was going down the drain.

I turned to Jones. "Bob," I said, "that rain is too much. You don't have to go out there."

"No, Ernie," he said. "I made a promise. I'm going to keep it."

We did the interview under an umbrella, which didn't help much. By the time we got back to the locker room, we were soaked. I never forgot the thoughtfulness of Bob Jones. Of all the people I have met in sports, he was the best.

Originally printed on April 8, 2003.

Whatever you called Lohrke, he was lucky

Baseball fans always have been fascinated with players' nicknames, but the one nickname most significant to me belonged to Jack Lohrke, an infielder with the New York Giants when I broadcast their games in the early 1950s. His nickname was "Lucky."

Our Giants radio and television broadcasts were sponsored by Chesterfield cigarettes. Chesterfield's No. 1 rival was Lucky Strike, sponsor of the Brooklyn Dodgers broadcasts.

The Chesterfield/Lucky Strike rivalry was so bitter and intense that the Chesterfield folks would not allow me or my partner, Russ Hodges, to call Jack Lohrke "Lucky." All the other announcers and writers could use that nickname, but not us.

(Incidentally, when the Giants played their spring training games in Phoenix, in the shadow of Camelback mountain, our sponsor would not allow any reference to the mountain because of that other dirty word, Camel.)

I wouldn't mention all this except for Jack Lohrke. He was a player who came by his nickname legitimately. No nickname ever fit like this one.

Jack was spared death when the bus carrying the entire Spokane team spun off a mountain road, killing nine and injuring eight. It was the heaviest loss suffered by a professional baseball team.

The Spokane Indians were on the way to Bremerton, Wash., in 1946 when the team took a rest stop at Ellensburg. A message awaited manager Mel Cole, who was to inform Lohrke to report immediately to the San Diego Padres of the Pacific Coast League. Jack shook hands with his teammates and started hitchhiking south.

Fifty miles east of Seattle, the Spokane team bus careened off the road and tumbled down the Snoqualmie Pass. Nine passengers, including manager Cole, were killed. Forever after, Jack Lohrke — the man who missed that bus — was known as Lucky Lohrke.

Jack had been just as lucky in an earlier accident, but at that time there was no publicity and no nickname. After World War II, Lohrke was a private first-class on an Air Force plane from Camp Kilmer, N.J., to San Pedro, Calif. He was seated on the plane, ready for takeoff, when an officer came aboard and usurped the seat.

The plane went down on that flight. All were killed.

"I was really mad when that officer bumped me off the plane," Lohrke recalled. "But I'm thankful now that he saved my life."

During World War II, Lohrke landed at Normandy with the 35th Infantry Division and later fought in the Battle of the Bulge. U.S. forces suffered heavy losses, but Jack escaped without a scratch.

He came home after the war, played one year in the minors and joined the Giants in 1947. He played with the New Yorkers five seasons, then finished his career with two more years for the Phils.

I remember Jack Lohrke as the guy who was truly Lucky — even if we couldn't call him that on the air.

Originally printed on June 10, 1994.

Celebrating the underdog and human spirit

At the movie theater last weekend, something happened that I hadn't seen in a long time. When "Seabiscuit" faded from the screen, a spirited round of applause sounded through the auditorium. The audience seemed to appreciate and enjoy the wholesome story of a scrawny, cast-off horse who fought huge odds to become a champion.

The film took me back to those days of the Great Depression — an era I lived through. Twenty-five percent of the nation's workforce were without jobs. It was a hard existence for many. Sports were a welcome diversion in the national gloom. There were four major sports — baseball, boxing, horse racing and college football.

As much as I loved sports, my interest in the horses was confined to the great characters from the track in Damon Runyan's stories. Later, when I was broadcasting Orioles baseball, an owner of a prominent Baltimore stable named a horse Ernie Harwell. The horse started racing at Bowie and Pimlico. Although a betting favorite in his maiden race, he finished out of the money. A few races later he bowed a tendon, and the owner kept dropping him into lesser races. He won a few times on minor tracks, then headed for the glue factory.

When I saw "Seabiscuit," it brought back memories of those days around the track. It reminded me again what a tough business thoroughbred racing is. The movie's strength is its celebration of the human

43

spirit. It's the comeback story of a discarded, runty horse and three broken men who put their lives back together.

When I left the theater, I thought about a speaker I once heard. I don't remember the time or place or even the speaker's name. Addressing a group of 100 or more, he held up a $50 bill and asked his audience, "Would any of you like to have this money?" Hands were raised. Then he crumpled up the bill. "Do you still want it?" All the hands again went up.

Next he dropped the $50 and ground it into the floor with his shoe. He picked up the crumpled and dirty money. "Now who still wants it?" The hands — all of them — went up again.

"You've learned a lesson," he told his audience. "No matter what I did to that money, you still wanted it because it did not decrease in value. Many of us are crumpled and ground into the dirt by our mistakes. We feel worthless. But no matter how much you are beaten up, you never lose your value. Dirty or clean, neat or crumpled, you are still priceless to those who care about you.

"Don't ever forget that the worth of our lives is measured by who we are. You are special."

Originally printed on July 30, 2003.

Too harsh on baseball? Maybe because we care

"I'm not spending my hard-earned money to watch overpaid millionaire baseball players." I've heard that statement too many times. Yet I've never heard a movie fan say, "I'm not paying to watch an overpaid millionaire actor." And I've never heard a similar excuse about a rock concert.

This contrast in public attitude cuts deep into our American psyche. As youngsters, most of us played baseball. We dreamed of big league stardom. At the sandlot level it's a simple game. Many of us have said, "If I were a big leaguer, money wouldn't matter. I'd be happy to play for almost nothing."

Movies and music are different. Since few of us can act or sing, we have deep admiration of those who can. Somehow it doesn't bother us that Bruce Willis or Sylvester Stallone can be paid $20 million a movie. Or that Barbra Streisand demands $10 million for one concert. We are willing to separate the performances of entertainers from any jealous feelings about their overinflated incomes.

There are other factors in the comparison. The worth of entertainers can be defined easily by the box-office value. Few players have made a difference in ticket sales. In baseball, the player is the product, and it's hard for the fans to make a judgment about his worth.

Baseball players suffer in public opinion because of their predecessors. Fans remember that the greats of former years were paid only a pittance compared to today.

The modern players move from team to team more often. This free-agency system hurts fan loyalty because the players don't stay with one team long enough to gain or deserve support.

Compared to other pro athletes, baseball players are highly criticized.

Football, basketball, hockey, golf and tennis produce millionaires. Yet the public accepts these other athletes with much less complaining.

Why? I think it's because baseball is deeply ingrained into our culture and we are more sensitive about its problems.

Maybe we are more critical of baseball because we care more about it.

Originally printed on August 27, 1999.

Here's to no strike during crisis

In a fervent surge of patriotism, baseball players and owners have vowed to support America's war effort.

Yet we've heard no promises from labor or management to forget their differences and extend the present contract during our national crisis. Instead, rumors abound that after the season, all the patriotic fervor will give way to a confrontation over salary caps, revenue sharing and other issues.

If such squabbling continues during these perilous times, I say: "A pox on both of their houses."

History reminds us that when money and baseball mix, nothing should surprise us. For instance, our national pastime barely dodged a damaging scandal during World War I, escaping disgrace only because its most important figure was drunk.

Despite the war, the major leagues continued in 1918, but stopped the regular season after Labor Day. The Cubs and Red Sox met in a hurriedly planned World Series. But the players were not happy. For the first time, pennant winners had to divide World Series shares with other first-division teams. Because of poor attendance, there was little money to share. Just before Game 5 in Boston, the players threatened to strike.

Baseball in those days was ruled by a three-man National Commission. Its most powerful member was Ban Johnson, the American League president. A strong, iron-willed ruler, he was baseball's man to

47

stop the strike. But Johnson didn't even know there was a strike. He had been drinking all morning in a Boston bar and was drunk.

He arrived late at the ballpark. The stands were filled with fans, but no players were on the field. He quietly met with the player representatives, Les Mann of the Cubs and Harry Hooper of the Red Sox. The mood was ugly. Even though America was at war, the players refused to play. The fans were getting impatient. Already the game's start had been delayed. A wrong move here would not only end the World Series, it would create a lasting scandal.

And the big boss of baseball was drunk.

Johnson tried to pull himself together. Assuming an air of judicial dignity, he turned to Hooper. "Harry," he pleaded, "do you know what you will do to the good name of baseball if you don't play?"

Before the player could answer, Johnson flung his arm around Hooper's shoulder. "Go out there," he bellowed. "Your fans are waiting."

Hooper looked helplessly at Mann. The players shrugged. It was plain that Johnson was in no condition to discuss anything, so the teams took the field. The Series went on, and scandal was averted.

But had Johnson been sober and able to talk, there might have been a bitter confrontation and a strike. So baseball was saved because its most important man had too much to drink.

Originally printed on Octoboer 2, 2001.

Baseball Chapel part of Hall of Famer's legacy

Two former Phillies entered the Hall of Fame this week. One was a slugger — third baseman Mike Schmidt. The other was the ultimate singles hitter — outfielder Richie Ashburn.

I never saw Schmidt play many games; but I followed Ashburn closely in my days of broadcasting in the National League. And I was proud to be a member of the Veterans' Committee that voted him into the Hall of Fame last winter.

For some reason, Phillies fans never appreciated Schmidt; but they loved Richie, whom they have established as a sort of Mr. Phillie. And certainly most baseball fans all around the country look on Richie as a true Phil. Yet, he did play for two other teams, the Cubs and the Mets. He finished his career with the Mets and was their only All-Star in 1962, their first season.

His two years with the Cubs (1960-61) were undistinguished except for one special contribution. Richie reminded me of it when I saw him a week or so ago at Veterans Stadium in Philadelphia.

"I don't believe anyone realizes it," he told me. "But I helped the Baseball Chapel get started. Some of the Cub players came to me, as the player representative, and asked me to set up a meeting for a Sunday morning speaker to come to the hotel and conduct a church service. I did that. Randy Hundley, Don Kessinger and some of the others served doughnuts and coffee. We did some praying and conducted the kind of service that developed into Baseball Chapel."

Under the guidance of Jim Kaat and Al Worthington, the Twins were starting to do the same thing. Bobby Richardson led a similar group with the Yankees. In Detroit, sports writer Waddy Spoelstra began to organize another. I remember those early Tiger meetings; sometimes only Waddy, I and one or two players would attend. In 1973, Spoelstra obtained official sanction for the Baseball Chapel from commissioner Bowie Kuhn.

From the chapel services have come the development of weekly Bible studies for many teams. Jeff Totten is the Tigers' Bible teacher. The players and their wives meet with Jeff and his wife, Karla, have lunch and conduct a lively dicussion at a local restaurant.

The chapel program has spread to the minors. Now 140 minor league teams have services. And similar chapels are conducted in pro football, basketball, golf, auto racing and bowling.

It all goes back to those days in 1960 when some of the Cub players wanted a speaker for Sunday morning.

Originally printed on August 3, 1995.

The good,
the bad,
the ugly tie

Great scouts deserve place in Hall of Fame

irdie Tebbetts did just about everything in baseball. He was a player, coach, manager, general manager and scout. I think scouting was Birdie's true passion. Even in the last few seasons before his death in 1999, he loved to be at the ballpark with his stopwatch and clipboard.

Birdie was a great conversationalist. Frank and outspoken, he always had an opinion. I can't think of anyone I enjoyed listening to more. Birdie's last crusade was Hall of Fame recognition for the scouting fraternity. Pounding away at the importance of scouts in baseball, he certainly converted me to his cause.

During my two terms on the Veterans Committee, Tebbetts was one of its most respected members. And his experience with that group gave him further insights into the Baseball Hall of Fame.

Besides honoring players and managers, executives and umpires, the Hall of Fame also has special wings for writers and broadcasters. Scouts certainly deserve a place, too. An astute executive like Dave Dombrowski of the Tigers will tell you that good scouting is the backbone of player development. If you don't find the good talent, you can't build a strong farm system.

Baseball's first scout probably was Harry Wright. In the early 1880s he traveled from the East to California to discover Tom Brown and Jim Fogarty, who became big league stars. Until 1909 there were no full-time major league scouts. However, there were many tipsters. Barbers, bartenders and ex-players always were spotting phenoms for their favorite teams.

Most baseball historians credit Larry Sutton of the Dodgers as the first full-time scout. Sutton discovered 11 of the Brooklyn 1916 league champions.

Many other great scouts followed. Among them were Charlie Barrett, Paul Krichell, Tom Greenwade, Joe Devine, Cy Slapnicka, Joe Cambria, Jim Russo and Howie Haak.

Scouting isn't easy. Although the guys who judge talent are wrong 95 percent of the time, they still keep their jobs.

"We scouts have to judge a 17-year-old and project what he will be when he reaches 23," an old-timer told me. "We have instincts to help us make that judgment, but who can tell how much a youngster will develop over a six-year span?"

The Hall of Fame does have an excellent display about the business of scouting. Some day, maybe the folks at Cooperstown will do even better and finally recognize the tremendous contribution scouts have made to baseball.

Originally printed on August 2, 2003.

ERNIE HARWELL

Puckett's place in shrine rooted in his love of game

"**A**re you going to Cooperstown for the induction ceremonies?" That's a question I've been asked many times in the past week. And the answer is, "No, I'm not going." I always miss that wonderful event. I don't want to give up a broadcast. The first rule in radio is: "Don't leave your microphone. You might lose your job to the guy who replaces you."

But Sunday's induction is one I would love to see, because one of my favorite players — Kirby Puckett — is becoming a Hall of Famer.

Puckett has many great attributes. He pulled himself out of the Chicago ghetto to become a superstar. And even when his outstanding career was cut short by irreversible retina damage in 1995, he never complained, but showed us an admirable outlook about baseball and life.

All of us appreciated the bouncing youthfulness of Kirby's play. He truly enjoyed the game. It showed in the verve and spirit he brought to the diamond.

Except for the 1981 strike, Kirby might never have become a big leaguer. During the strike, Jim Rantz, the Minnesota Twins' farm director, had time to see his son in a college game in Illinois. Puckett's play for the opposing team caught Rantz's eye, and the Twins drafted Puckett No. 1 in January 1982.

Puckett made it to the majors in 1984. After only 21 games with Toledo, he was ordered by the Twins to report to Anaheim for a game against the Angels.

His plane landed late in Los Angeles. "I knew nothing about L.A.," Puckett said. "So I told the cab driver to take me to the ballpark in Anaheim. The tab was $85. I had a lot less than that in my pocket. I told the cabbie to wait. I went into our clubhouse, borrowed the money, and took it to him."

Puckett then made his debut, going 4-for-5, stealing a base and scoring a run.

In his first year, Puckett did not hit a home run. But coach Tony Oliva taught him to keep his weight back and drive the ball. He ended his 12-year career with 207 homers.

What a thrill it was to see those Puckett circus catches in centerfield. And we will never forget his World Series heroics — especially in Game 6 in '91. He robbed Atlanta's Ron Gant of an extra-base hit and banged out a single, triple and home run. The homer, off Charlie Leibrandt, gave the Twins an 11-inning victory. They won Game 7, 1-0, on Jack Morris' 10-inning seven-hitter.

From ghetto to stardom, Puckett loved to play the game, and showed it. He certainly deserves to be in the Baseball Hall of Fame.

Originally printed on August 4, 2001.

Take notice: Palmeiro on path to Hall

Now that Rafael Palmeiro has hit his 500th home run, he is no longer baseball's best-kept secret. Until this year, Palmeiro was more famous for his Viagra commercials than for baseball. He just went on being a humble, quiet and overlooked star.

At 38, Palmeiro is a marvel. He has never been on the disabled list in his 17-year-plus career. He has the smoothest, most balanced swing in the game. He is a classy fielder, but he has won only three Gold Gloves because flashier first basemen have attracted more ballots. He has never led a league in hitting, home runs or RBIs. He has never been named MVP. Although he is a truly great star, Raffy always has been overshadowed by a famous teammate.

When the Cubs sent him to Texas after the 1988 season, the Rangers' MVP candidate was Ruben Sierra. In Baltimore, Cal Ripken was the headliner with his iron-man streak. The Orioles didn't want Raffy enough to keep him, and he made his way back to the Rangers. But even on his second tour of duty at Texas, he has been overshadowed — first by Ivan Rodriguez, MVP catcher, and now by baseball's best player, shortstop Alex Rodriguez.

Palmeiro's first team — the Cubs — gave up on him early. After Raffy's first full season, general manager Jim Frey and manager Don Zimmer didn't think he had hit with enough power. Also at the time, the Cubs needed a closer and were eager for Mitch

Williams. Palmeiro had hit .307 his first full season, but with only eight home runs and 53 RBIs. In December 1988, Palmeiro went to Texas and Williams headed for Wrigley Field. There were seven other players in the trade. The Rangers also got Jamie Moyer and Drew Hall. Curtis Wilkerson, Steve Wilson and minor leaguers went to Chicago. Only Palmeiro and Moyer are still in the majors.

It was three years after the trade before Palmeiro discovered power. In 1991 he hit 26 homers for Texas. Since then he has never hit fewer than 22. He signed as a free agent with Baltimore in '94 but returned to Texas in 1999. Raffy says he wants to play another three years. He is certainly healthy enough to do it. Three thousand hits is a reachable goal. He entered this season with 2,634. Only three other players have 3,000 hits and 500 homers — Willie Mays, Hank Aaron and Eddie Murray — all Hall of Famers. Certainly, the once-overlooked Raffy is on his way to Cooperstown.

Originally printed on May 14, 2003.

Many on deck to replace Ted as game's living icon

Now that Ted Williams has died, who will succeed him as baseball's living icon?

Ted was larger than life. His fame transcended baseball. What former superstar will equal the scope of Williams' influence? Whose death could attract such sweeping media coverage?

No baseball figure has ever matched Babe Ruth as an icon. Even in an era of less-intense media coverage, the Babe was not just a player. He was a worldwide celebrity.

Throughout baseball history, each era has boasted a super superstar. In the early 1900s it was New York Giants right-hander Christy Mathewson. Matty was the first college graduate to become a baseball idol. He was clean-living, intelligent and highly talented. Honus Wagner and Ty Cobb also grabbed headlines. Wagner was a fantastic fielder and hit with power. Cobb, a fiery genius in spikes, was the game's first millionaire. After Ruth came Joe DiMaggio and Williams. Then Willie Mays, Nolan Ryan, Mark McGwire, Sammy Sosa and Alex Rodriguez.

But who can replace Williams as baseball's senior statesman?

I might leave out somebody, but let me give you some choices:

- **Yogi Berra:** Who is better known to the casual fan or to anyone outside the game? Certainly, nobody has been quoted more.

- **Bob Feller:** He had a fabulous pitching career. Like Williams, he gave up baseball to serve his country in active, wartime duty.
- **Stan Musial:** A great hitter who was to St. Louis what Williams was to Boston. No one has a more charming personality than Stan the Man.
- **Mays:** Considered by many the best modern player. But Willie's Say Hey luster has dulled during retirement. His post-career attitude has soured many in the game.
- **Ryan:** The great strikeout artist who is somewhat the darling of the advertising folks.
- **McGwire:** Colorful home run champ. His retirement is probably too recent to put him in the elder statesman ranks.

There are others who might be considered as Williams' successor. How about Sandy Koufax, Hank Aaron, Ernie Banks, George Brett or Reggie Jackson?

It won't be easy to find our man. Williams was a lightning rod for headlines and a prime candidate for celebrity status even years after his playing days ended. Can anybody replace him?

Originally printed on July 19, 2002.

300-victory club
full of tough competitors

When Roger Clemens joins the 300-victory club, he will bring with him a special quality that has characterized all club members — an intense, competitive instinct. I didn't know all these great pitchers, but the ones I knew were tough competitors.

There was Warren Spahn, for instance. Spahn's history as a strong competitor is tinged with a touch of irony. Pitching in spring training for the Braves in 1942, Spahn refused to brush back Pee Wee Reese despite orders from manager Casey Stengel. Because of the refusal, Stengel thought his rookie left-hander lacked guts and shipped him to the minors.

Then came World War II. Spahn fought with the Army in the Battle of the Bulge, one of the toughest tests in military history. He won a battlefield commission, a Purple Heart and a citation for bravery under fire. Afterward, nobody questioned his courage.

Spahn returned to win more games (363) than any other left-hander in history. When he got No. 300 in 1961 at the age of 40, his catcher was Clemens' present-day manager, Joe Torre. After the victory, Spahn autographed the catcher's mitt for Torre, then 21. Torre shipped the mitt home for safe-keeping, but hasn't seen it since.

Lefty Grove was probably the toughest competitor of the 300 club. Grove once caught me in an on-the-air mistake and confronted me in an irascible way. In referring to the first game ever at

Cleveland's Municipal Stadium, I had said, "In that first game, Mel Harder of the Indians beat Lefty Grove and the Red Sox, 1-0."

Several years passed before I saw Grove.

"You got that score all backwards, you dirty so-and-so," he told me. "I won that game, not Harder."

It might not sound like it, but Lefty and I were good friends.

Another tough guy in the 300-winner class was Early Wynn. It took him eight tries before he reached the goal. Somebody asked Wynn how many times he would try for his 300th.

"I'll keep on until somebody cuts the uniform off me," he said. "And whoever comes out to the mound to do it had better bring somebody with him."

Wynn's philosophy of toughness was reflected in another quote: "Yes, I will throw at any hitter crowding the plate — even my mother." Wynn once held up a tiny match pad for the umpire.

"Take a look at this," Wynn shouted. "That's the size of your strike zone when Ted Williams is hitting."

Gaylord Perry was another 300-game winner who used every wile possible. He and the umpires were in constant arguments about his so-called spitball. Perry posed as a picture of innocence, but the umpires knew better. Before he won his 300th, Gaylord ordered 100 custom-made Seattle jerseys. His plan was to sell them for $1,000 each. After each inning, Perry ducked into the clubhouse and put on a new jersey. His scheme was a flop because even avid collectors wouldn't go for the overpriced items. They sold like hotcakes — last year's hotcakes.

Originally printed on May 30, 2003.

Williams' wisdom is splendid as ever

Ted Williams was talking, and when Ted talks, I listen.

"The two greatest players I saw were Joe DiMaggio and Willie Mays," he said.

"Which one was better?" I asked.

"I won't pick one over the other. But if I were an owner I'd be happy with either one."

I asked Williams for his appraisal of modern hitters.

"I don't denigrate the hitters of today like a lot of other old-timers," he said. "They are certainly bigger and stronger and hit the ball farther than we did. But they don't get enough walks. Many of them are too impatient."

What's the secret of good hitting?

"Getting a good pitch. The good hitter won't swing at the pitcher's pitch. Joe Cronin was great with his advice about that. He always said, 'Make that sinker-baller come up.' Or he might say, 'He's throwing hard and high. Make him come down.'

"A lot of hitters today get the good pitch, but they are over-anxious and foul it off."

"What about the pitchers today?" I asked Williams.

"They don't have the control of the old-timers," he said. "They get behind in the count too often. The best control pitchers I hit against were Ernie Bonham of the Yankees and Fred Hutchinson when he pitched for Detroit."

"What did you look for when you studied a pitcher?" I asked.

"First off, I wanted to know about his fastball. I asked my teammates who had batted against him and how hard he threw. After that, I knew I could adjust to all of his other pitches."

"Who was the best pitcher you ever faced?"

"Bob Feller," he said. "I thought Bob Gibson was tops later on, and you can't leave Sandy Koufax off the list. Tommy Lasorda told me that of all the pitchers he knew, he'd pick Koufax for that one big game he had to win."

Williams has a campaign to get Shoeless Joe Jackson into the Hall of Fame.

Jackson had a .356 lifetime batting average but was tainted by the Black Sox scandal.

"The judgment on Jackson was too harsh," Williams said. "He was in court twice and never convicted. Judge Landis banned him for life. Joe paid for his mistake many times over. Others did worse things and were never punished. Some of them are even Hall of Famers."

Williams asked me about Detroit's new park. I told him it would be more pitcher-friendly than Tiger Stadium, but centerfield would not be as deep.

"That's OK," he said, "if they make the fence out there high enough. That old park was great. I sure loved to hit there."

Ted, 80, keeps busy with his baseball museum in Hernando, Fla. His enthusiasm and his love for the game have never waned.

Originally printed on May 7, 1999.

Not-so-burning question:

Is it better to open at home or on the road? It's not a discussion that will lead to peace in the Middle East or rid the free world of terrorists. But as part of the arcane baseball clubhouse patter, the subject can assume a degree of importance.

The not-so-burning question: Is it better to open the season at home or on the road?

I sampled some Tigers' opinions, and here they are:

- **Steve Sparks:** Give me a home opener anytime. I like the added electricity of being in our own park, cheered by our fans.
- **Al Kaline:** I liked it better when we opened on the road. When I played, I liked starting on the West Coast in warm weather. By the time we reached Detroit, we'd already played a couple of games in warm weather and we felt ready.
- **Damion Easley:** Open at home. It's more comfortable. It's a place where you can relax. I have a home in Detroit, and that's where I want to be when we get the season under way.
- **Jack Morris:** I wanted to open the season wherever the domed stadium was. No wind and 72 degrees. Of course, that meant on the road.
- **Dean Palmer:** I definitely would rather open on the road. It gives you a chance to get into the swing of things, back into a routine before you get home. You want to be at your best for the home debut. There are more distractions at a home

opener. More media and more undue attention. It's good to play a game or two before you have to face that.

■ **Juan Samuel:** I prefer to open at home. As a coach or player, you want to get there and get settled in. It makes a difference to get everybody going.

■ **Matt Anderson:** I'd rather open on the road. There are fewer distractions there. When I was younger, it was difficult to find a place to live in Detroit, get adjusted and be ready for Opening Day.

■ **Shane Halter:** Opening on the road has more pluses. There you have a chance to spread your wings and get going. Then you are more relaxed and ready for the home opener.

■ **Phil Garner:** I have a slight preference to opening on the road. I think a lot of players get too hyped for any opener. It's better to get rid of that edginess on the road. Better to get that anxiety out of your system. Also, some players coming to Detroit for the first time find it hard to adjust and locate a place to stay. If we open on the road, the wives and family can go ahead to Detroit and find a place.

The final results in the unofficial Harwellian poll: road 6, home 3.

Originally printed on April 1, 2002.

Players, owners should listen to Aesop

Iusually don't like to write about a subject that might take away the focus from baseball's playing field. But today I'm compelled to address the strike.

Baseball is a great survivor. Its resiliency always has enabled it to bounce back from strikes and all the other slings and arrows tossed its way by owners and players. But I think the next strike will kill the game as we know it today. Even its specter is harmful, but once the real thing happens, watch out!

Throughout its history, baseball has been battered by selfishness and greed. More than a hundred years ago, owners and players battled. Owners imposed an iron will on the players, who revolted and formed new leagues. During World War II, with Americans sacrificing their lives overseas, the Red Sox and Cubs threatened to stop the World Series unless their share of the payout was increased.

We've seen strike after strike. Nobody remembers the issues and no settlement ever seems to solve the problems. Arbitration, free agency, salary caps, haves and have-nots — all such talk only baffles the person on the street. The perception is that two groups of millionaires are fussing over how to divide their millions. It's difficult to relate to either side.

Let's not give up. Maybe some owners or players will come to their senses and realize how much the game needs harmony and peace. Maybe they will realize that baseball is the greatest game of all and that a little compromise from each side can keep it that way. Let them hear the cry of the fan and preserve the game.

I submit some required reading for each side.

This is from the ancient fables of Aesop, who always gave us stories with a moral:

"One day a countryman going to the nest of his goose found there an egg all yellow and glittering. When he took it up, it was as heavy as lead and he was going to throw it away, because he thought a trick had been played upon him. But he took it home on second thought, and soon found to his delight that it was an egg of pure gold. Every morning the same thing occurred, and he soon became rich by selling his eggs. As he grew rich he grew greedy; and thinking to get at once all the gold the goose could give, he killed it and opened it only to find nothing.

"Greed oft o'er reaches itself."

Originally printed on August 3, 2002.

September is cruel to some

Unless his team is in the pennant race, September is a hard, cruel month for a major league baseball player. The game-to-game grind is wearing him down. He longs for the end of the season, dreaming of relaxing with family and escaping from the pressures of his profession.

If he's a veteran, September is the month that brings thoughts of retirement. Often, by spring those thoughts have vanished, but sometimes he decides that he has had enough and quits.

"I quit because I struck out four times in one game against Tony Cloninger — all on fastballs," Yogi Berra said. "That one game told me I didn't have it anymore."

Ted Williams retired after hitting a home run in the final at-bat of his career. Ted's blow came Sept. 26, 1960, off Baltimore's Jack Fisher before a Fenway Park crowd of 10,454.

Williams had announced his retirement in a magazine article after the 1954 season — six years before that dramatic home run. That was the year he suffered a broken collarbone in spring training and then contracted pneumonia during the regular season. Still, he batted .345 in 117 games.

Another star's retirement involved a magazine article. After the 1956 season, Brooklyn superstar Jackie Robinson sold his story to Look magazine. But before the piece could be published, the Dodgers traded Jackie to the New York Giants. He refused to report and never played again.

Injuries forced Tigers manager Alan Trammell to quit as a player in 1996. "I was hurt most of the season and played only 66 games," Trammell recalled.

"In late July I had surgery on a left ankle bone spur and went on the disabled list. Reactivated in September, I played only three or four games. With all the kids coming up from the minors and the team going nowhere, I decided to retire. I played the final game against Milwaukee and went 3-for-5. In my last at-bat I faced Mike Fetters. I hit a line-drive single through the box — the same kind of hit I had in my big league debut."

"Hanging it up" became a literal reality for Gene Mauch, the longtime major league manager, when he retired as a player. In 1958, Mauch was a playing manager for the Minneapolis Millers in the American Association. One night he made three errors and went 0-for-5. After the game, he summoned the clubhouse boy.

"Son, get me a hammer and some nails," he said. Then Mauch proceeded to take off his shoes and nail them to the wall above his locker. That was his farewell to the playing field.

George Brett enjoyed a much happier retirement day at the end of the 1993 season. In his final game, all of Brett's teammates paid tribute to him by wearing their trouser legs high. They also wrote Brett's No. 5 on their socks.

George singled in the eighth inning to drive in the tying run. He left for a pinch-runner and never played again.

Originally printed on September 19, 2003.

Fewer games would boost playoff drama

P ostseason baseball used to be simple. Not any-more.
Once there were two eight-club leagues — the American and the National.

Winners in each league met in the World Series. Now each league has three divisions. So before the World Series, there is a best-of-five division series featuring the winners of each division and a wild-card team.

Next come two best-of-seven league champi-onship series. After that, the best-of-seven World Series.

The playoffs are a good idea. They keep more teams in competition. But they have become unwieldy. There are too many games in each series. I realize that the system is television-driven. Still, it would be much better for the division and league championship series to be best-of-three series. I might even advocate a one-game playoff for the divi-sion series. There is nothing more exciting than one game — do or die.

Before the playoffs, baseball often used to enter September with the pennant races almost over. For instance, the Yankees would have a 15-game lead with maybe 20 or 30 games left. The race was set-tled, and the other clubs played out the string.

Now there are usually several divisions enjoying a close race in September.

And with the wild card in the mix, even more

cities get involved, and interest runs high right up to the playoffs.

The playoffs have come a long way. Buddy Blattner and I broadcast the first one in American League history in 1969. Opening at home, the Baltimore Orioles won two close games, 4-3 and 1-0. Then they finished off the Twins with an 11-2 victory in the only game at Minneapolis.

None of the three games sold out. We broadcast on the Hughes Sports Network, a forerunner of ESPN. For some reason there was no broadcast that year of the National League playoffs.

I like the wild card. I like the playoff system. Yet I think that interest in the playoffs has diminished the importance of the World Series. There are too many games before we reach the Series. But baseball has never learned that less can be more, and television keeps insisting on more games. So it will always be this way.

Originally printed on October 1, 2003.

Tackling the issues

With the baseball season nearing the All-Star break, too much attention has been focused on peripheral issues rather than on actual diamond action. There are four in particular:

Roger Clemens' Hall of Fame cap; Sammy Sosa's doctored bat; irrational fan behavior; and the commissioner's decree that the winning league in the All-Star Game gets home-field advantage in the World Series.

All of these issues have been overblown. With the numerous sports talk shows, ESPN and emphasis on investigative reporting today, there is a lot more of beating a dead horse in our business than in the past.

Here is my take on these questions:

The All-Star Game home-field issue: This is an idea I don't like. I'm in favor of an All-Star team playing to win, but this is not the answer.

Let's view the issue from the standpoint of the player. He'll play hard and try to win anyway — that's his nature.

But of all the teams in the pennant race and the subsequent playoffs, who knows which will meet in the World Series? And does any player have more than passing interest in whether his league will win the championship?

I don't think so.

Clemens' cap: Most observers have overlooked the fact that the Baseball Hall of Fame does not demand that a player wear a certain cap. It meets with him, hears his preference and makes a decision, usually agreeing with the player's choice.

Also, the Hall is not an official part of baseball. It is an independent museum and the guardian of the artifacts and history of the game. When Wade Boggs received a $25,000 signing bonus from Tampa Bay by promising to wear a Devil Rays cap into the Hall, the folks at Cooperstown felt they had to guard against such a travesty.

I think the best solution would be for the Hall of Fame to eliminate caps and depict a bareheaded inductee on each plaque. But there would be a problem. All Hall of Famers now wear caps, and bareheaded newcomers would destroy uniformity.

Sosa's corked bat: Sammy made a mistake. Yet, this felony will not besmirch his lifetime reputation — as some commentators have insisted.

I can cite at least three recent Hall of Famers who were not disgraced by diamond misdeeds. I am thinking about George Brett and his pine-tar bat, Gaylord Perry and his spitter, and Jim Bunning, who cut balls with his belt buckle. Bunning survived not only to make the Hall, but to become a U.S. senator.

Irrational fan behavior: There have always been spasms of fan goofiness — even before the present era of exhibitionists striving to appear on television.

I remember when fans threw pop bottles, charged into umpires' dressing rooms and even set fire to grandstands.

Such actions are wrong. I don't condone them. But the answer rests in better security and sterner punishment for offenders.

Originally printed on July 7, 2003.

Cold weather unavoidable in long season

Does anybody out there have an answer to bad weather?

The baseball folks certainly don't. With all the snow, ice and rain this spring, they are moaning and shaking their heads as they seek a solution to the age-old problem. Believe me, there isn't an answer. You can't do a thing about it. Even openers have been rained out this season. And when the teams do play, they have to fight the windchill and snowflakes.

I remember when some people used to say, "Baseball starts too early. The schedule-makers should begin the season a week later."

Well, the Tigers' early start — the first March Opening Day in Detroit — didn't seem to hurt.

In fact, the weather was much better than a week or two later. All things considered, you have to concede that it really doesn't make much difference. We could still get snow in May or June.

Although the weather around here is much better in October than in April or May, playing baseball then just can't happen.

All the other sports are in full swing, and baseball's leaders also have lengthened the season and playoffs so much that a World Series would probably end at Thanksgiving.

So the answer is: Let 'em play baseball in April and let 'em freeze.

There is really nothing new about cold weather

and baseball around here. In my photo collection at the Detroit Public Library is an action shot of Davy Jones of the Tigers batting in a snowstorm in the final opener at old Bennett Park.

The year was 1911. And remember the famous Arctic explorer Frederick Cook?

After his expedition into the Earth's coldest region, he attended a 1909 World Series in Detroit. But he left in the fourth inning and returned to his hotel to escape the cold.

A lot of folks left even earlier than the Arctic explorer during the first game at Comerica Park — the 2000 opener. I have never experienced more miserable weather for baseball. If it had been just an opener, the game would have been postponed because of rain, snow and sleet. But because it was also the opening of the park, it had to be played. Most fans in the sellout crowd left before the second or third inning.

Sometimes, the game must go on — no matter what the conditions. And nobody has figured out an answer to the bad weather.

Originally printed on April 18, 2003.

Stealing signs not new to baseball

I always thought stealing signs in baseball went with the franchise.

That's why I was startled to learn San Francisco Giants manager Dusty Baker had accused Montreal Expos manager Felipe Alou of stealing signs.

Since the Baker accusation, I've talked to numerous players, coaches and managers; all were surprised at Baker's protest.

"It's all part of the game," was the consensus.

There was an ironic twist to the Baker-Alou confrontation. Before the Giants series, the Expos met to go over their signs. Mark Grudzielanek had missed a hit-and-run sign in a loss to the Padres.

"We're missing our own signs," Alou said. "We certainly aren't concerned about stealing signs from the other team."

Sign stealing has been around forever. For years, the Chicago White Sox were accused of using scoreboard lights to flash knowledge to their hitters. More recently, the Tigers were suspicious of shenanigans at Toronto's SkyDome.

"A couple of years ago we suspected the Blue Jays were getting our signs," Tigers third baseman Travis Fryman said. "They were using a centerfield camera, flashing a red light for a curve and a green light for a fastball."

Kansas City Royals manager Bob Boone remembers a game when he was catching for the Angels.

"We're playing the Indians in Cleveland and Bobby Bonds, their hitting instructor, is whistling every time Jim Slaton, our pitcher, throws a fastball," Boone says. "Between innings I asked our pitching coach to watch me and check to see if by some mannerism I'm tipping off Slaton's pitches.

"By the third inning, Bonds is still whistling and he's correct on every pitch. So I go to the mound and say to Slaton: 'They're still getting our signs. I'm not giving you anymore signals. Just throw what you want and I'll catch it.'

"He went all the way to pitch a real good game. Slaton is still mad at me because I caught everything he threw even though I didn't know what was coming.

"A couple of years later Johnny Goryl, the Indians third-base coach, told me he was getting my signs and relaying them to Bonds in the dugout."

Originally printed on May 23, 1997.

Blame Torre and Brenly for All-Star ugly tie

Ties don't work in baseball. On its way to an exciting finish, the 2002 All-Star Game ended in a 7-7 deadlock and left nobody happy.

Though most of the fans and media have jumped on commissioner Bud Selig's bones, he is not entirely to blame. My finger is pointed at the managers. Couldn't Bob Brenly and Joe Torre have planned to save pitchers in the event of extra innings? It used to be that way. Seven games in All-Star history had gone into extra innings, and all produced winners.

Selig was caught in an untenable situation. The managers ran out of pitchers. Why the announcement was made after the first half of the 11th and final inning is a mystery. Before the final inning would have made more sense. Or it might have been better to let the public address announcer explain in detail after the final out.

As tough a decision as Selig faced, what about this hypothetical one? The game is tied. One manager has another pitcher ready in his bullpen, but the other manager has used his quota and can't continue. Does the manager who planned well get penalized with a tie?

Another question: Why eliminate the MVP? For the first time, this award would honor Ted Williams. Then, because of the tie, no MVP was selected. I think even a tie game can produce a most valuable player.

Some critics suggest that the roster be extended for the All-Star Game. To me, this only makes matters worse. Just let the managers plan better. Also, I don't agree with the policy of having to use every player. Sure, it's tough on the players selected, but let's put winning first.

Another rule I don't endorse is the one that each team must have at least one representative in the game. Let's name the best players, and if a team doesn't have a true All-Star, it doesn't deserve representation.

The only other All-Star tie happened in 1961. I broadcast that game at Fenway Park in Boston, and there was no big to-do about the lack of a winner. After nine innings, it rained for 30 minutes. Skies cleared, but there was confusion about returning or calling the game. Many players had early flights to rejoin their teams. So the game ended in a 1-1 tie. I don't remember any protest from fans or media about the decision.

Originally printed on July 12, 2002.

How 'bout them Tigers?

Tigers' history shines in Kuenzel's photos

It was summer in the mid-'60s. The voice on my phone said: "I've had no success with the Tigers. I want to sell them some photographs, but they won't listen. I know that you're a collector. Would you be interested?"

"What do you have?" I asked.

"My dad was a friend of photographer Bill Kuenzel. He used to go to Tigers games and help him. Before Kuenzel died, he gave my dad hundreds of great photos."

I knew about Kuenzel, Detroit's first sports photographer. "Bring me some of those pictures, and I'll take a look," I told the caller.

In less than a week I was admiring a real treasure — a collection of photos from 1901 to the mid-'50s.

"Kuenzel got these pictures together in 1950 and took them to Tigers owner Walter O. Briggs, with the idea that the Tigers could publish them in an anniversary book," the photos' owner told me. "Briggs turned him down and Bill gave all the photos to my dad. Now, they are mine. Would you like to buy them?"

"Yes," I told him." But they are worth much more than I can offer. If you sold these photos separately, you could make a lot of money."

Despite the caveat, he took my offer and delivered the collection to me. Into scrapbooks, Kuenzel had put 8-by-10s of every World Series from 1905 until the mid-'50s. He also had compiled books of photos of different teams, individual shots of all the great stars and many, many other photographs. Their quality is outstanding. For instance, there's a photograph of managers Frank Chance of the Cubs and Hughie Jennings of the Tigers in a home-plate conference before Game 1 of the 1908 World Series. The photo's clarity makes you believe the shot was taken yesterday. Kuenzel's ability shines through in this photo and all the others.

As a pioneer in Detroit photographic history, Kuenzel is a story in himself.

At 14, he sold his first picture to the Detroit News — a shot of a Ford automobile on Grand Boulevard on July 21, 1899. He became one of the first full-time newspaper photographers in 1901, when he was 17. He took Detroit's first sports action photo that same year. Kuenzel was at Bennett Park when Ty Cobb broke into the major leagues in 1905. In 1909, when Cobb was accused of intentionally spiking Frank Baker of the Athletics in a slide into third, Kuenzel's action photo of the play exonerated Cobb.

It was Kuenzel who invented the famous "Big Bertha" camera used by every newspaper photographer in the first 50 years of the 20th Century. Kuenzel worked for the News for 52 years. He died in 1964, two years after his retirement.

I was fortunate to find that great treasure trove of Kuenzel photos through a random phone call. When I donated my baseball collection to the Detroit Public Library in 1965, the Kuenzel photographs were a part of that gift.

Originally printed on September 1, 2003.

Tigers will never reach depths of 1899 Spiders

If misery loves company, Tigers fans should extend a welcome to the Cleveland Spiders of 1899. No matter how bad the Tigers are, they will never sink to the level of the Spiders. That I can guarantee.

The Spiders won 20 games and lost 134. They were so terrible that after only 24 games at home, they had to finish the season on the road. Their home attendance for the season was 6,088.

Strangely, the Spiders were a fairly decent team before 1899. They had taken over the disbanded Detroit National League team after the 1888 season.

But in 1899 they hit bottom, soon after Frank and Stanley Robinson, the Spiders owners, bought the bankrupt St. Louis Perfectos. The Perfectos hardly lived up to their name. In 1898, they finished 39-111, in 12th place, $63\frac{1}{2}$ games behind the champion Boston Beaneaters.

The Robinson brothers switched 11 Spiders players to St. Louis, including three future Hall of Famers (Cy Young, Bobby Wallace and Jesse Burkett). Manager Pasty Tebeau also went along. The Spiders received nine Perfectos players and then filled out the roster with anybody they could find.

Here are some of the reasons the Spiders established themselves as the worst team in baseball history: The ace of their pitching staff was Jim Hughey, who won four games and lost 30. His ERA was 5.41.

Charlie Knepper lost 22 games.

The others in the rotation were Frank Bates (1-18), Crazy Schmit (2-17) and Harry Colliflower (1-11). The Spiders' leading hitter was manager Joe Quinn, who batted .286 but did not hit a home run in 147 games. Four players shared the team's home run leadership with two apiece. The entire team hit 12 homers.

These losers were no better in the field. Harry Lochhead made 81 errors at shortstop. Leftfielder Dick Harley made 27. Among the regulars, only Tommy Dowd committed fewer than 20 errors. His total in centerfield was 17.

When the season started, the Spiders' manager was Lave Cross. He lasted 34 games, winning eight and losing 26. Cross was replaced by the Australian native Quinn, an undertaker in the off-season. How appropriate was that? In late August, the Spiders reached their depth. They lost 24 games in a row and dropped 40 of the final 41.

The Spiders' final game epitomized their season of disaster. A cigar store clerk named Eddie Kolb dared Quinn to let him pitch against Cincinnati. The 19-year-old pitched the whole game, allowing 18 hits. He walked five and fanned one. The Reds beat him, 19-3.

Originally printed on June 27, 2003.

Tigers lucky Cobb trade failed

I have written about the greatest trade that never happened — Ted Williams for Joe DiMaggio. Now what about the greatest Tigers trade that never happened?

It has to be the one involving Ty Cobb in his early years, when Detroit almost lost the one player who, more than any other, has defined the Tigers' history.

Young Ty had played only one full year here when Tigers owner Frank Navin seriously considered trading him to Cleveland in March 1907 for a veteran outfielder named Elmer Flick.

Cobb had batted .320 the year before, but had been in fights with his teammates and was considered a very difficult player to handle. Flick had led the American League in hitting in 1905 and was a solid established star.

Tigers manager Hughie Jennings wanted to make the trade. Navin was willing to go along with him but, in a letter to his manager, he stated some reluctance.

From my collection at the Detroit Public Library, here is Navin's letter, dated March 18, 1907: "It seems hard to think that such a mere boy as Cobb can make so much disturbance. On last year's form, he has a chance to be one of the grandest ballplayers in the country. He has everything in his favor. It would not surprise me at all to see him lead the league this year in hitting and he has a chance to play for 15 years yet."

Navin was a good prophet. Cobb did lead the league in 1907, hitting .350. He played another 22 years — not 15.

"Flick is a dangerous man to bother with," Navin's letter continues, "for the reason that he has about all the money he cares for, does not care about playing ball, except as a means of livelihood, and is liable to quit on you at any time, besides being a great deal older than Cobb."

It was Cleveland that settled the issue. The Indians promptly rejected the trade because they felt Cobb was too much of a troublemaker.

Cleveland's rejection was the best thing that ever happened to the Tigers. The aging Flick hit .302 in 1907 and retired three years later. Cobb sparked the Tigers to a pennant for three straight years and went on to become the greatest player in the club's history.

The Tigers found out in March 1907 that sometimes, the best answer of all is, "No."

Originally printed on June 25, 2002.

Some Tigers starred as All-Stars

With the All-Star Game coming up, let's look at its history from a Tigers perspective. Detroiters have not had much impact on the game in recent years.

But some do stand out in All-Star records.

Charlie Gehringer has the highest lifetime batting average in All-Star history (.500). Gehringer played in six games with 10 hits in 20 at-bats. He also has the highest on-base percentage (.655).

However, the most active Tigers All-Star is Al Kaline. He was selected 18 times and played in 16 games, hitting 12-for-37 for a .324 average, No. 10 on the list.

In the pitching department, Jim Bunning shares the most-games record with Juan Marichal, Don Drysdale and Tom Seaver. Each pitched in eight. Although Bunning started with Detroit, he ended his career with the Phillies.

Sparky Anderson also boasts All-Star distinction. He, Alvin Dark and Dick Williams are the only three to manage All-Star Games in both leagues. Anderson led the National Leaguers in 1971, 1973, 1976 and 1977, and the 1985 American Leaguers.

There are six major leaguers who have represented four teams in All-Star games. One is Tigers third baseman George Kell, who played in the All-Star Game with Detroit, Boston, the Chicago White Sox and Baltimore. The others are Roberto Alomar, Lee Smith, Kevin Brown, Walker Cooper and Goose

Gossage.

Sometimes guys make news by not playing in the All-Star Game. Three eventual American League MVPs did not make the team. Neither did six National League MVPs. Two of the American Leaguers have Tiger connections. Hank Greenberg was shunned in 1935, despite his 25 home runs and 101 RBIs at All-Star time.

In '35, the managers of the previous season's pennant winners picked the 20-man teams — a custom that lasted until 1947 when fan voting began. So, Greenberg can blame his own manager, Mickey Cochrane. Cochrane selected Lou Gehrig as his first baseman and used another first baseman, Jimmie Foxx, at third.

Gehrig was hitting .322 with 11 homers and 40 RBIs. Foxx was batting .313 with 13 home runs and 50 RBIs.

Juan Gonzalez is another overlooked Tiger, his rejection coming in 1996 when he was AL MVP with Texas — before he joined the Tigers. The other bypassed AL MVP was Robin Yount of the Brewers in 1989.

Six National League MVPs were not All-Stars: Don Newcombe, Dodgers, 1956; Dave Parker, Pirates, 1978; Willie Stargell, Pirates, 1979; Kirk Gibson, Dodgers, 1988; Terry Pendleton, Braves, 1991; and Chipper Jones, Braves, 1999.

In his entire career, Gibby was never an All-Star. In his MVP year, he hit 25 homers for the Dodgers with 76 RBIs and a .290 batting average. He stole 31 bases in 35 tries. The same season, Gibby became a World Series hero with his game-winning, two-run homer off Oakland's Dennis Eckersley in Game 1.

Yes, some Tigers made it big in All-Star Games, but some of their big guys didn't make it at all.

Originally printed on July 10, 2003.

Streaky years nothing new for the Tigers

I s this a streaky season or not?

From their 0-11 start, the Tigers have streaked through the season, with more losing streaks than winning streaks.

I wasn't around when the Tigers set their record for consecutive victories. They did it twice, in 1909 and 1934, winning 14 straight each time. I did broadcast their games when they established a team record for consecutive losses. That happened during the 1975 season. From July 29 through Aug. 15, they dropped 19 straight. Ralph Houk was the manager. The club lost 102 games and held the club mark for losses in a season until Buddy Bell's team dropped 109 in 1996.

Houk's 1975 team was leading the league at the end of April, but soon fell apart. By August the Tigers were in complete disarray. The losing streak ended Aug. 16 at Anaheim, when Ray Bare pitched a two-hit shutout. I remember the Los Angeles Times said the next morning, "With a chance to break a league record, the Tigers choked and won a game."

Another time in Anaheim, it was quite different. The 1984 Tigers won their 17th straight road game when they beat the Angels on May 24 at the Big A. These were Sparky Anderson's pennant winners who were in first place at the start of the season and stayed there for the entire season. Their 35-5 start ensured that no other club even came close. The team was the talk of the sports world, and Sparky was featured on every sports page and every television show. The Tigers were riding high.

At the peak of Sparky's prominence, he and I were having breakfast at the hotel coffee shop in Anaheim. A fan came up to our table.

"Hi, Sparky," he said. "Great to see you. You've always been my favorite manager. I'm from San Diego, but I used to live in Cincinnati and was a big Reds fan. You are the very best. There's never been a manager as good as you."

Anderson nodded his head and concentrated on his eggs.

"And, by the way, Sparky," the fan continued. "What are you doing these days?"

After the Tigers won their 17th straight road game that night, they flew to Seattle to play the Mariners in a three-game series. The Mariners played like champs and swept the streaking Tigers.

Originally printed on June 13, 2002.

ERNIE HARWELL

Simon's got that swing

In the big band era, one of the musical hits was "It Don't Mean A Thing If You Ain't Got That Swing."

That could be Randall Simon's theme song. The Tigers slugger has that swing. Such a good one that wherever he has played, batting coaches and other hitting gurus have told him, "Don't ever change. Just keep swinging."

Simon's simple approach: "I just want to get a pitch and go for it," he said. "Nobody taught me to hit. When I get to the plate all I think about is hitting the ball hard. I can hit anybody. No matter who's on the mound."

Chided about not drawing walks, Simon dismisses such criticism with a shrug and a smile. "That doesn't bother me," he said. "I didn't come all the way from Curacao to the States to takes pitches. I'm up there to swing."

Simon was the youngest of 11 children. He was surrounded by five sisters and five brothers. When Simon was 2, his father left. His mother, who will be 70 in October, supported the family by cleaning homes, and washing and ironing clothes.

The boys played in the backyard, hitting bottle caps with broom sticks. The sisters watched, cheering on their brothers. The boys couldn't afford balls or bats, but sometimes would make a ball from an old sock. "We'd dampen the sock to harden it and then throw it at a strike zone we painted on the house," Simon said.

HOW 'BOUT THEM TIGERS?

On his 12th birthday, Simon's mother gave him his first glove. Before that, he never played on a team. He joined the Little League, where his hitting soon attracted attention. His high school had no team, so Simon was a star on the sandlots. Because of his swift progress, he signed with the Atlanta Braves at the age of 16.

Batting coach Don Baylor told Simon: "Just do what you are doing at the plate. You wouldn't be here if you weren't doing it right." Simon also got a boost from Hall of Famer Willie Stargell. "I like your swing," Stargell told him. "That's the way I used to hit. Swing hard and hit the ball hard."

When he joined the Tigers, Simon heard the same advice from batting coach Merv Rettenmund. "Just keep it simple," Rettenmund told him, "and keep on swinging."

Originally printed on September 20, 2002.

Garner remembered fighter in Mansolino

C hallenging your boss-to-be is not the best way to land a job, but it worked for Tigers coach Doug Mansolino.

In the summer of 1993, Doug Mansolino was the first-base coach for the Chicago White Sox. His team was amid a simmering feud with the Milwaukee Brewers, managed by Phil Garner. After a hit batsman, Garner unleashed a tirade toward Mansolino in the coach's box.

Having trouble hearing the stream of invectives over the crowd noise, Mansolino glared toward Garner and shouted: "Are you talking to me?"

"Yes, I am. I'm talking to you," Garner retorted.

Mansolino — all 155 pounds of him — charged the dugout, confronting Garner and his players.

"On my way to the dugout," Doug recalled, "I ran into the plate umpire. He was coming over to try to stop the fight. I slugged him in the throat and then went into the dugout after Garner. I grabbed him, got in a quick punch, and then all hell broke loose."

Let's fast-forward to the winter of 1997. Mansolino was home in Clovis, Calif., unemployed and sorting job offers. He had left the White Sox, and in the previous summer had managed the Class A Capital City team in the South Atlantic League. One morning his phone rang.

"Hello," he answered.

"Doug, this is Phil Garner. How are you?"

"I'm OK. What's going on?"

"Jim Gantner, our coach, is retiring and I need a guy to replace him. I thought about you. Would you take the job?"

The answer was yes. Mansolino began the 1998 season as Garner's first-base coach. On Aug. 11, he switched to third. He continued coaching at third base in 1999 for Phil, and when Garner came to Detroit last season, he brought Mansolino with him.

"He'd always impressed me," Garner said. "He had a great background in education and a wonderful reputation as a top baseball instructor. Then when I saw him in action during that fight, I admired his character and his courage. He wasn't afraid of anything or anybody. He was coming into our dugout ready to take on me and everybody else."

Mansolino, 44, has a tremendous passion for baseball. As a teenager from a broken family he lived in his car, pitched batting practice for the Los Angeles Dodgers, cleaned houses, worked in gas stations and served tables. He still managed to play baseball in high school and college and gain a bachelor's degree from California State Long Beach and a master's degree in education from Cal State Dominguez Hills. In pro baseball he has managed, coached and served as a director of minor league instruction. Three times he has traveled to Korea to teach the game he loves.

Though he never played a game as a professional, he has the confidence of all who know him and have worked with him. It's ironic that this well-educated and respected coach won his present job by challenging the man who would hire him.

Originally printed on April 13, 2001.

Mantle's 535th homer was a gimmie

It was a meaningless, desultory game, but it highlighted a defining moment in Tigers history — Mickey Mantle's 535th home run, off Denny McLain on Sept. 19, 1968, in Mantle's last visit to Tiger Stadium.

Like other baseball lore, the event has assumed a life of its own, perpetuating myths and untruths.

The three principals in this drama were McLain, Mantle and catcher Jim Price. Since Mantle is dead and McLain is busy rehabilitating himself, I asked Price to tell the behind-the-plate story. In his words, here is the story:

"We'd clinched the pennant and then had a rainout. McLain was going for his 31st win. We were leading, 6-1, in the eighth. With one out and nobody on, here came Mantle. It was his last time at-bat.

"I walked away from the plate to give Mantle center stage. The Tiger players and the crowd gave him a standing ovation. Before he pitched, McLain called me to the mound and said, 'Hey, let's let him hit a home run.' I looked at Denny and said, 'That's a great idea.'

"McLain smiled. 'Ask him where he wants the pitch,' he told me. When I returned behind the plate, I told Mantle, 'He wants you to hit a home run, so tell me where you want the pitch.' Startled, Mantle looked back at me.

" 'He's serious,' I reassured him. Mantle looked at Denny, who nodded his head and grinned. Then

97

Mantle said to me: 'High and tight.'

"McLain pitched, and Mantle, still skeptical, took it for a strike. Next he hit a foul line drive to right. After that, Mantle looked at Denny and stroked his hands across his letters. McLain delivered. Mantle drilled one into the rightfield upper deck. As Mickey rounded second, Denny had a big grin on his face and began to clap his hands. Crossing the plate, Mantle turned to me and said, 'Thanks.'

"It was a thrill to me because Mickey had always been my hero. When the media later asked Denny if he had grooved the pitch for Mantle, he told them, 'No, I really didn't groove that pitch.'

"Nobody ever asked me. I never said anything about it.

"Years later after Mantle was quoted at a banquet, saying McLain grooved the pitch, I told the story. It's the only time I ever tipped off a batter with the location of the next pitch."

Originally printed on June 6, 2003.

ERNIE HARWELL

Batting champ Alexander not so great with glove

Did you know the Tigers once dealt away a player who won the American League batting title the same year they traded him?

His name was Dale Alexander, also known as the Big Ox or Moose, two nicknames denoting his lack of fielding ability.

In 1932, Alexander became the only American League batting champion to play for two teams in one season. Still, he is almost unknown in Detroit. He was hitting only .250 in June when the Tigers traded him and Roy Johnson to the Boston Red Sox for aging outfielder Earl Webb. Alexander hit .372 the rest of the season. Competing against Babe Ruth, Jimmie Foxx, Lou Gehrig, Charlie Gehringer and Al Simmons, he finished at .367 and won the batting crown.

Why did the Tigers give up on the Big Ox? His iron glove. Alexander's fielding lapses at first base drove manager Bucky Harris crazy. Also, the team wasn't going anywhere (the Tigers finished fifth, 29½ games behind the champion Yankees), so changes were in order.

There was never any question about Alexander's hitting ability. He batted .380 and hit 31 home runs for Toronto of the International League in 1928. The Tigers grabbed him, and he started with a bang. In his rookie season, 1929, he banged out 215 hits and batted .343. He set what were then American League records for most hits by a rookie and also

99

most triples by a rookie (15). The next two seasons he hit .326 and .325. Then he won the batting title in 1932.

His success was short-lived. The 1933 season — and his first full year with Boston — was his last. He suffered a leg injury, and infection set in. Alexander had to quit baseball because he never recovered from the injury. With modern medical methods, his leg could have healed and his career been prolonged.

The trade that sent Alexander and Johnson to Boston for Webb turned out to favor the Red Sox.

Like Alexander, Johnson was a poor fielder. He twice led the league in errors. As a Tiger in 1929, he set the still-standing AL record with 31 outfield errors. But at Boston he hit better than .300 for three straight seasons. Then for the final three seasons of his career with the Yankees and the Boston Braves, he was just an ordinary hitter.

Webb did little for the Tigers. He played only 87 games for Detroit in 1932, the year of the trade. After only six games in 1933, the Tigers traded him to the White Sox, and after 58 games with them, his career ended.

The big man in the deal turned out to be the almost unknown Tigers hero, Alexander. He became the only American Leaguer to win a batting title while playing a season for two teams.

Originally printed on September 14, 2001.

Comerica is a beauty; don't change a thing

After watching the first 16 Tigers homes games, I have fallen in love with Comerica Park. It's a great place to watch the best game of all — baseball.

I've heard rumblings that the fences might be moved in. Don't let it happen. I like the expansive areas. The distances from the plate to the fences are fine.

Let's keep them that way.

Already suffering from a severe case of home run-itis, baseball doesn't need another band-box ballpark. The home run is fine — in its place. But it has become too common and lost its significance.

Comerica Park will yield homers, but they will have more meaning and importance. Showing that the park is not home run-proof, the Red Sox hit five in one game. The big sluggers will get their share, but the Punch-and-Judy hitters won't be slapping drives over the fences, like they do at Camden Yards and the other undersized parks.

In a big place like Comerica Park, the game will be better. Pitchers will challenge the hitters. They won't aim for the corners and give up a lot of walks. In turn, the hitters more often will go for the first pitch. We'll see fewer walks, and the game will move along at a faster pace. Also, there will be more hits up the alleys — more doubles and triples. We'll enjoy exciting baserunning, relays, tag plays and more true baseball.

HOW 'BOUT THEM TIGERS?

I say to Comerica Park the same words the song-writer wrote: "Stay as sweet as you are. Don't let a thing ever change you."

Other features I like about Comerica: Watching a game while walking around the ballpark. The statues of the all-time Tigers greats. ... The gigantic scoreboard in leftfield. ... The food courts, featuring all kinds of cuisine. ... The comfortable radio booth and spacious press box. ... The great food service in the press area from Bridgetta Sims, press lounge coordinator; Daniel Lee, executive chef; and Homer Wiley, assistant chef. ...

The historical displays of the Tigers through the decades. ... The oversized clubhouses. ... The interview rooms. ... The lighted Tigers atop the scoreboard. ... The carousel and Ferris wheel. ... The neat infield surface and the beautiful outfield green. ...The centerfield flagpole, still in fair territory.

I especially like the way the architects have separated the baseball part of Comerica Park from the added attractions. When you take your seat to watch the game, it is strictly baseball — no distractions from all the extras. Yet if you're not an avid fan, you can visit the other attractions just to enjoy a day at the park.

Comerica Park is great. Let's keep it that way.

Editor's note: Since this column was printed on May 19, 2000, the leftfield fence was moved in. For the first three seasons at Comerica, the leftfield power alley was 395 feet. It was shortened to 370 feet in the spring of 2003.

Nixon snubbed Tigers, but he made up for it

When Richard Nixon died, several writers said he was the most avid baseball fan among presidents. Those stories reminded me of an embarrassing non-visit the Tigers had with Nixon at the White House.

It was just before the All-Star Game in 1971 at Tiger Stadium. The date was July 9. Baseball's hottest star that year was Vida Blue, the Oakland Athletics' left-hander. By the All-Star break, Blue had won 17 games and was grabbing headlines all over the country. Nixon, the ultimate baseball junkie, had entertained Vida and his teammates at the White House.

U.S. Sen. Bob Griffin of Michigan thought that his Tigers should have equal time. So, he set up a meeting. The whole Tiger team was to visit the White House and meet the president.

At least, that was the plan.

First, the senator and his staff entertained all of us with a terrific luncheon in the Senate dining room. Manager Billy Martin, his coaches, Jim Campbell, Doc Fenkell and Vince Desmond were there. Also along were Jim Hawkins of the Free Press, TV announcer Larry Osterman, my partner Ray Lane and I.

After some picture-taking, the group went to the White House. Sen. Griffin led us around to the Rose Garden.

"Wait here," he told us. "I'll go get the president

and he will come out here and visit with all of you."

The senator went into the White House and we waited. We must have steamed in that hot sun 30 or 35 minutes.

Finally, Sen. Griffin returned with an embarrassed look on his face.

"I'm very sorry, gentlemen," he said. "The president very much wanted to come out and meet with all of you, but is working on an important speech and won't be here. He asked me to give you his best regards."

The Tigers were angry.

Sure, they should not be at the top of White House priorities, but a five-minute visit from the president would not stop the world from turning. Besides, hadn't Nixon recently taken a lot of time to entertain the A's? And hadn't this meeting with the Tigers been scheduled months in advance?

Griffin was even more frosted than the team by Nixon's snub. But he kept his best political face through the rest of our visit.

However, several weeks later, each one in our traveling party received through the mail a baseball autographed by Nixon.

Originally printed on June 24, 1994.

Short story became an epic with Trammell

S ince 1901, 28 players have been regular Tigers shortstops — from Norman (Kid) Elberfeld to Chris Gomez. A look at the list emphasizes how Alan Trammell has dominated this position.

Trammell is completing his 19th year with the Tigers, all but the past two seasons as a full-time shortstop. The nearest to him in longevity is Donie Bush, with 13 Tigers seasons. Then comes Billy Rogell (eight years), Harvey Kuenn (five), Dick McAuliffe (four) and Ed Brinkman (four).

There is no doubt that Alan is the king of Tigers shortstops. Until 1920, Bush was the best at short. He won the job on the 1909 American League champions and stayed until 1920. Donie went to Washington on waivers and managed the Senators in 1923. He also managed Pittsburgh (where he won the pennant in 1927), the White Sox and the Reds. Donie put in 16 years as a major league player with a lifetime average of .250 and nine home runs.

In the late '30s, selectors began to list Rogell as the best shortstop in Tigers history. During eight years as the fulltime shortstop, Rogell solidified the championship infields of 1934-35. He also spent two terms with the Red Sox, one year with the Cubs, and ended his 14-year career with a .267 average and 42 homers.

The next standout shortstop was Kuenn. Certainly, he was the best hitter.

Kuenn led the American League in 1959 with a

.353 average, then was traded to the Indians for Rocky Colavito. Harvey was not a great fielder, and after his fifth year at short, the Tigers switched him to the outfield.

Kuenn also played for the Giants, Cubs and Phillies. He managed the 1982 Milwaukee Brewers to a pennant. In 15 years as a player he had a .303 average with 87 homers.

McAuliffe was the next standout at short. He played there four years and switched to second base in mid-career. Dick batted .247 in 16 years with the Tigers and Boston. His home run total was 197.

Another fan favorite was Brinkman, who came to Detroit from Washington. He was probably the best fielder among Tigers shortstops. He had little power and did not hit for average, but Ed was the steadiest of them all. He put in four years with the Tigers, 1971-74.

Tommy Veryzer followed Brinkman. Tommy never lived up to his early billing, playing only three years before Trammell took over.

Now the shortstop is Gomez. The young man from California surprised many as he quickly demonstrated that he belongs in the big leagues. He was Tigers rookie of the year in 1993 and last season took over at short from the king, Alan Trammell.

We all consider Chris a little guy. But this present-day shortstop at 6-feet-1 is a giant compared to the Tigers' incumbent in 1901, Elberfeld. The Kid was 5-5½ and weighed 134 pounds. From the Kid to Chris it has been a long parade, but the best in Tigers history has to be Trammell.

Originally printed on September 23, 1995.

Champion '68 Tigers belong on top 10 lists

"You done splendid."

That's what Baseball's No. 1 anti-grammarian, Casey Stengel, would have said about HBO's "A City on Fire: The Story of the '68 Detroit Tigers."

I agree with Casey. The documentary, airing this month on HBO, is excellent. Producer Dan Klein deftly handled a subject that could have courted disaster. His balanced approach avoided exaggerating the team's contribution to civil harmony, and he was evenhanded in presenting the racial issues of the 1967 riots.

As a baseball man, I most enjoyed the review of the Tigers' World Series victory.

Giving the Series its due, Klein devoted almost half of the presentation to the Tigers' triumph, a feat that somehow has never gained its rightful place in baseball history, generally ignored on the list of outstanding World Series. For instance, this spring my good friend Bill Madden of the New York Daily News picked the 10 best World Series. He omitted 1968. I agree with his No. 1 pick (the 2001 classic between the Yankees and Diamondbacks), but I would have listed the '68 classic somewhere among the 10.

To state the case for the '68 World Series, let's see what made it unique:

It was the last time two true pennant winners met in a series. Beginning in 1969, each team had to qualify by winning a playoff series.

To get his star outfielder, Al Kaline, into the line-up, manager Mayo Smith made a bold move, switching centerfielder Mickey Stanley to shortstop and benching light-hitting defensive star Ray Oyler.

The opener matched Denny McLain, Detroit's 31-game winner, against Cardinals ace Bob Gibson, who had won three games in the previous Series and boasted a 1.12 ERA for the '68 season. Each was the Cy Young and MVP winner. Gibson set a Series strikeout record, fanning 17 in Game 1.

In Game 2, Mickey Lolich hit a home run — the only one he'd ever hit in sandlot, high school, minor leagues or any level of baseball. Playing in the only World Series of his career, Kaline hit .379 with two home runs and eight RBIs.

The Tigers, down three games to one, rallied and won the final three games.

Willie Horton's throw to nip Lou Brock at home plate in Game 5 turned the Series around. Smith let Lolich bat for himself in the seventh and Mickey delivered a clutch hit.

In Game 6, the Tigers tied a record by staging a 10-run third inning to rout the Cards, 13-1. Jim Northrup sparked the surge with a grand slam. The Tigers' win set the stage for a tense Game 7 — Lolich against Gibson, each aiming for his third win of the Series.

Northrup's seventh-inning triple broke a scoreless tie and sent the Tigers to their championship — a fitting climax to a great World Series.

Now, doesn't it deserve a higher place in baseball history?

Originally printed on August 9, 2002.

A lifetime
of memories

Some of my fondest times in game were with catchers

A colorful parade of catchers has marched through my baseball life. Here is a look behind the mask and chest protector of the most memorable from that unique and demanding position.

My most horrifying memory involved a catcher named Jumbo Barrett of the Memphis Chicks. Atlanta's Nick Cullop slid hard into Barrett and broke Jumbo's leg. Even from the stands I heard the bone snap. An ambulance sped to home plate to take Jumbo to the hospital.

Only a few days earlier, the Boston Braves had announced they were calling up Barrett to the major leagues. But the broken leg ended his career. He never played again.

I was only a young fan when I saw the Barrett tragedy. When I was a writer for the Sporting News in the mid-'30s, I met a lean Texan who was one of the game's unique characters — Paul Richards. Paul joined the Atlanta Crackers as a catcher. When I attended my first spring training as an announcer in 1941, he had become the Atlanta manager. In 1943 he returned to the big leagues with the Tigers. I wrote my first Free Press article about that event.

Richards was complex. He spit out profanities at umpires, but he was a daily reader of the Bible. He was very impatient but a great teacher — especially of pitchers. Paul hated the media, yet he was sports editor of his hometown paper.

110

When he managed in Baltimore we became very close, and I learned more baseball from him than any other insider. We played a lot of golf together. He died in what he would have considered the ideal setting — in his golf cart at the 18th hole on his home course in Waxahachie, Texas.

Another catcher who meant a lot to me was Brooklyn Dodgers Hall of Famer Roy Campanella. Campy came to the Dodgers the same year I arrived.

Roy had started in the Negro leagues at age 15. Although he was roly-poly, he was quick and had a great arm. In 10 seasons he was MVP three times, made eight All-Star teams and led the Dodgers to five pennants. An auto accident in 1957 ended his career and put him forever in a wheelchair. He never lost his smile or optimistic outlook.

We played a lot of hearts together on those long Dodgers train trips. Later we served on the Hall of Fame Veterans Committee. He was always the same sweet guy with the hearty disposition.

The next catcher on my list — Clint Courtney — was a sharp contrast to Campy. He was as mean and combative as any player I've ever known.

"Scrap Iron" was an apt nickname for him. A feisty little tobacco chewer, he was constantly fighting. And he wouldn't back down to anybody. Never mincing his words, he was open and direct. He was once asked during a radio interview:

"For whom were you traded in that White Sox deal with Kansas City?"

"Oh, they got a couple of rinky-dinks like me," Courtney said.

I knew him best at Baltimore, where he caught for

the Orioles. Often, we'd go to the racetrack together. He was the wildest horse bettor I ever knew.

With the Washington Senators, the tough little guy was stricken with an inability to toss the ball back to his pitcher. After a lot of agonizing and hard work he finally overcame the problem.

Courtney was managing Richmond when he met an ironic death. The tough competitor died in the clubhouse playing Ping-Pong.

I saved two of my best for last — Bill Freehan and Lance Parrish.

These Tiger greats were very much alike. They were leaders of championship teams — Bill in 1968 and Lance in 1984. Each came to Detroit highly touted and each lived up to his advance billing. As players, Bill and Lance conducted themselves with a quiet dignity — they were hard-nosed competitors, but off the field were true gentlemen.

Keen intelligence, a love for the game and great team spirit — these were the qualities that I admired in Freehan and Parrish.

I knew them best in Baseball Chapel. Freehan was the chapel leader when we began the program. Later, Parrish — as a player — was a faithful member and now is a strong leader and much-appreciated teacher.

Over the years, I've developed a great regard for catchers — especially Tigers catchers. The one now in the radio booth with me — Jim Price — has a keen insight into baseball and has taught me a great deal about the game.

Originally printed on April 2, 2001.

Lost Babe autographs cost an arm and a shoe

It was March 1930, in Atlanta. I was 12 years old. The Yankees were playing their way north from spring training. I sneaked down to the front-row box seats at Ponce de Leon Park, and when Babe Ruth came off the field, I begged him for an autograph.

"But, kid," he said, "you ain't got no paper. What am I gonna sign?"

"My shoe," I told him. I held my leg over the railing and shoved my foot toward him. I was wearing dirty Keds (the Great Depression equivalent of today's Nikes).

"OK," he laughed. "I'll do it." And sure enough, he signed my shoe.

That old tennis shoe vanished years ago to the land where old tennis shoes go to die.

Twenty years later I got another Babe Ruth autograph. And I don't have that one either.

This happened in 1950. The Babe had been dead two years. But in my collecting efforts I had met a lady named Ruth Frymir in New Haven, Conn. She started what was probably the first all-sports bookstore. Somebody had cleaned out the old Yankees office files and sold Ruth contracts and checks of the Yankees' players. I bought a contract of Johnny Suggs, a Yankees infielder who signed for $3,000 in 1922.

More important, she sold me a check signed by Babe Ruth. The check was dated May 31, 1922. It was in the amount of $4,398.86 (half a month's pay) and was signed by Yankees president Jacob Ruppert. Babe endorsed the check on the back.

Also on the back was a deduction. No, not withholding, FICA or insurance. The deduction was a $200 fine by American League President Ban Johnson.

The Yankees were playing at the Polo Grounds that year. Babe was called out on an attempted steal of second. He began to berate the umpire and was ejected. A fan in the box seats began to shout insults at Babe as he came off the field. Ruth got so mad that he vaulted over the railing and chased the fan. The fan had left so quickly to escape the Babe that he left his shoes at his box seats.

I kept that check for years and finally sold it. I regret that move because I realize how much that Babe Ruth autograph would be worth in today's market.

Yes, I had Babe's autograph twice — once on my shoe and once on his check. But they are both long gone.

Originally printed on August 10, 1991.

Committee is long gone, but memories will linger

ood-bye, Veterans Committee. I will miss you.
The Baseball Hall of Fame last week announced sweeping changes to its election process. The Hall disbanded the Veterans Committee and is giving former players a major say in who makes it to Cooperstown.

I enjoyed serving on the committee. Even though I'll be part of the new one, it will be a completely different experience. Last year — now deemed to be our final year — the committee consisted of 15 people. The new setup involves all the players who are members of the Hall of Fame, and all the writers and announcers who have been honored by the Hall.

Now the voting will be via mail. The former committee had discussions behind closed doors. We studied every candidate and leaned heavily on the opinions of those who had managed or played with (or against) the candidates. Sometimes their opinions from the field surprised us. I remember when Al Lopez told us that Nellie Fox, then up for election, was not the most valuable player on his 1959 White Sox pennant winners.

"I know of two or three of my players," Lopez said, "who contributed more to that team than Nellie."

Needless to say, this observation influenced our voting and we turned down Fox that particular year.

Although the meetings were secret, somehow Lopez's remarks were leaked to the Chicago press. That's why I feel justified in repeating them. They have long been on the public record.

The former committee often was accused of cronyism. There might have been some of that before I became a member. However, when I was in the meetings, I never detected the good-old-boy syndrome. I was always impressed by the way the members handled their duties. They came well-prepared for discussions, and the exchanges were sometimes spirited but always conducted with good feeling.

Many writers thought the old committee was not necessary. They contended that it was a slap at their selections because the purpose of the Veterans Committee was to give those rejected by the writers a second chance. To some extent, I agree with their point. Still, there were umpires, managers, Negro leagues stars and others to be voted on. And most of these were out of the scope of the writers' selection.

What I'll miss most about our committee is the wonderful dinner we had each night before our meeting the next day. To dine informally with those great stars and to talk baseball with Roy Campanella, Ted Williams, Yogi Berra, Pee Wee Reese, Hank Aaron and Bill White were super thrills.

Originally printed on August 18, 2001.

My television journey

Do you remember the first sport you saw on television?

The first for me was a football game — Giants vs. Eagles in Philadelphia. It was 1947.

At that time television of any kind was strictly experimental. I was broadcasting Georgia Tech football on the radio in Atlanta. A Tech alumnus who had some connection with the NFL invited Morris McLemore, the Atlanta Journal football writer, and me to go with him to New York to see this new sensation, television. We took the long train ride from Atlanta to New York. As I look back, it's hard for me to believe that we would go that far just to see a television presentation.

What we saw was most primitive. The Dumont network executives took us to a room in Manhattan, where they served us a buffet lunch and put this new creature on display. Greeting us were NFL commissioner Bert Bell and some of his PR people. A few of the NFL owners were there, too. Around the room were several television sets no larger than a bread box. Grainy, jumpy pictures showed us small, indistinct players doing their thing on the gridiron in Philly. I don't remember if we had sound. Maybe we did, but I can't recall hearing an announcer. Even so, it was impressive — new to all of us. We returned to Atlanta, marveling at this new development in sports broadcasting.

I didn't see baseball on television until the summer of 1948, when I went to Brooklyn to become a

Dodgers announcer. In my first year I was on radio only, but the Dodgers televised a few games with Bob Edge at the mike. The next season I shared radio and TV duties with Red Barber and Connie Desmond. Red had done the first Dodgers TV in 1939, but that was just a quick experimental shot. The Dodgers' on-the-air TV began in 1948.

When I telecast the Bobby Thomson home run in the final National League playoff game Oct. 3, 1951, on NBC, television was reaching coast-to-coast. There were millions of sets by that time. The technique was still primitive, compared to today's advancements, but this new baby in sports was beginning to step up and be recognized.

Since then, it has come a long way.

Originally printed on May 23, 2003.

Long winning streaks have no guarentees

O akland's amazing winning streak has shone the spotlight on the greatest winning streak in baseball history — the New York Giants' 26 straight in 1916.

This is one of my favorite records, and I've referred to it many times during my broadcasts. It's amazing because those Giants not only had a 26-victory run, they had a 17-game winning streak that season and still failed to win the National League pennant. They didn't even come close. They finished fourth at 86-66. Half of their victories came from the two streaks.

Without the streaks, the Giants were 43-66, which meant the streakiest winning team in baseball history lost almost two of three games the rest of the season.

The 26-game run began Sept. 7 and lasted through Sept. 30. All of the victories were at home. The Brooklyn Dodgers won the pennant that year with a 94-60 record, and the fourth-place Giants finished seven games behind.

I was broadcasting for the Giants in 1951 when they staged another winning streak. This time they won 16 in a row on their way to the pennant.

Before they started their streak, the New Yorkers were 13½ games behind the Dodgers in mid-August.

Giants fans had given up. The relaxed players thought they were playing out the string. Alvin Dark, Whitey Lockman and others played golf with me almost every day. As the final week began, the team had almost caught the leading Dodgers and only then did the Giants realize they had a chance to win the pennant.

Another streak of note was staged by the Chicago Cubs in 1935. They finished the season with 21 straight victories, then lost the World Series to the Tigers.

Charlie Grimm was the Cubs' manager that year. He and a Chicago writer were feuding. The writer criticized every move Charlie made and never gave him any credit. He was constantly on Charlie's case. After 21 straight victories, the Cubs lost. The writer confronted Grimm.

"Charlie," he said. "I knew you couldn't keep it going."

Originally printed on September 13, 2002.

All-Stars light thrilling memories

Here are some musings, memos and opinions about the All-Star Game:

Baseball's All-Star Game is the best of all the sports for two reasons: 1. It pits one true league against the other. 2. The rules are not altered for the event.

Rivalry between the American and National leagues is weaker than it used to be because the autonomy of each league has eroded. But at least they are still leagues and not just divisions.

Any changes to the All-Star Game have been minor. The 1981 players' strike stopped regular play that year. When the schedule resumed for the second half of the season, it started with the All-Star Game in Cleveland. Pitchers were allowed to pitch no more than two innings and rosters were expanded from 28 to 30 players.

There will never be a fair way to select players for the game. My proposal years ago was to have a three-tier system, with fans making up one segment of the voting; players, managers, coaches and umpires another; and reporters and play-by-play announcers the third. This method allows sponsor promotion for the public voting and still takes care of the so-called expert analysis from the field or press box.

The All-Star Game struggled early. Arch Ward of the Chicago Tribune suggested the idea (as an adjunct to Chicago's 1933 World's Fair) to commissioner K. M. Landis. Landis liked the idea, but many owners were against it. They finally approved the game — but for one year only.

After the American League won the first game, 4-2, the National Leaguers asked for a rematch. The game has been with us ever since.

I've broadcast three All-Star Games, and there has been a strange angle to each one. My first broadcast was in 1958 at Baltimore, the first game in which there was no extra-base hit. My next broadcast was at Fenway Park, Boston, in 1961 — the second of two All-Star Games that season. It rained and the game ended in a 1-1 tie, called after nine innings.

My friends in Toronto asked me to work on the Canadian network for the 1991 All-Star Game. Lulu and I took the train to Toronto but were five hours late because a freight train wrecked and we had to be rerouted. That game was special to me because I was the speaker for the Baseball Chapel. I spoke to the most superstars I'd ever seen in one audience.

I've attended other All-Star Games without broadcasting them. The most memorable was the 1949 game in Brooklyn — the first in which an African American appeared. It was an outstanding group — Jackie Robinson, Larry Doby, Roy Campanella and Don Newcombe. I also enjoyed the 1993 game in Baltimore. I attended that one to serve on a discussion panel about the history of baseball parks.

The All-Star Game always has been a terrific thrill for me. I heard the first one on the radio in 1933, and on Tuesday I'm headed to Milwaukee for the 73rd.

Originally printed on July 6, 2002.

Greatest deal undone: DiMaggio for Williams

A baseball adage has told us for years that often the best trade is one never made. The most fascinating of the near-misses has to be the Joe DiMaggio-for-Ted Williams transaction.

Talk about a blockbuster! That would have been it. One superstar for another. Imagine DiMaggio's right-handed power zeroing in on the Green Monster at Fenway Park. Or how about Williams aiming for that short rightfield porch at Yankee Stadium? Certainly, that one was a dream deal.

Well, we all know it never happened. Did it come close? All my career I have heard that the deal was made and then canceled. It's not a story you can prove, but a lot of people believe it.

I phoned the St. Louis baseball expert, Bob Broeg, who covered DiMaggio and Williams extensively and has written about baseball for more than 60 years.

"It's probably true, but I can't verify it," Broeg said. "Many writers maintain that it actually happened, but there is no way to know."

Here's the way the greatest trade didn't happen.

Sometime in the 1940s, Dan Topping, co-owner of the Yankees, meets with Tom Yawkey, who owns the Red Sox, at a New York sports watering hole, Toots Shor's restaurant. There's lively baseball talk and much drinking. As the late night fades into early morning, the baseball executives get friendlier and friendlier. So friendly, they decide they will swap their biggest stars, Joe DiMaggio and Ted Williams. It will be a one-for-one, straight-up deal. The transaction is consummated with a handshake. News of this headline-grabber will be released the next afternoon.

So far, so good. But then comes the kicker. Yawkey, after sleeping off the night before, has second thoughts when he awakens. He grabs the telephone and rings up his pal of the night before, Topping.

"Dan, it's all off," Yawkey says. "I've changed my mind."

So Williams stays with the Red Sox, and DiMaggio remains a New York Yankee until the end of his career.

Did Yawkey and Topping really agree to make that deal, only to have Yawkey cancel? We will never know, but most baseball people think the story is true.

If so, it certainly is the greatest trade that never happened.

Originally printed on June 5, 2002.

Childhood recollection comes close, but no cigar

For the past week, Tom Keegan, a New York Post sports writer, has been interviewing me for a book. I don't know why anybody would write a book about me, but that's OK. Anyway, the process got me thinking about the temptation to bend the truth and try to look as good as possible when being interviewed for publication.

It's simply human nature to try to put yourself in the best light. It's called spin, or revisionist history. I recall an incident from my boyhood in Atlanta.

Mr. Russell Bridges, the father of my friend Ralph Bridges, owned the Alkahest Celebrity Bureau, which booked famous lecturers. One of his speakers was Sir Winston Churchill.

This was during the Great Depression of the 1930s. Sir Winston was between jobs and picking up a few bucks lecturing in the United States. Mr. Bridges was a canny businessman without a great amount of funds. So when Churchill came to Atlanta, he stayed at the Bridges' home.

The neighborhood kids played baseball almost every afternoon. Our diamond was next to the Bridges' residence. One afternoon, I excused myself from the game to visit their bathroom. As I reached the bathroom on the second floor, the door was closed. I waited a few minutes in the hallway. Finally, the door opened and out came a squat, elderly man smoking a cigar. It was Winston Churchill.

"Cheerio, young man," he said with a smile.

"Never give up."

A few minutes later I returned to the game. Little did I realize that I had just encountered the great English statesman, whose courageous stand in World War II would save our world from the ravages of Adolf Hitler.

So much for spin.

The story is partly true. We did play ball at the Bridges' house. I did use the bathroom, and at one time Winston Churchill visited the home.

But the statesman and I never met. Oh, we could have. It would have made a better story. And I could enhance our encounter even more. I could have talked with him, and the great orator might have been sympathetic to the fact that I was tongue-tied in my youth. Maybe he even encouraged me with a few kind words.

Really, there is no end to revising history once you get started. There is one problem. Truth gets in the way. And as the English poet Coventry Patmore once wrote: "The truth is great and shall prevail."

Originally printed on August 11, 2001.

Mantle first champ who switch-hit

Baseball never had a switch-hitting champion until Mickey Mantle batted .353 for the New York Yankees in 1956. That was the year Mantle won the Triple Crown, hitting 52 home runs and driving in 132 runs. His best career average came the next season when he hit .365 (the highest average of any modern switch-hitter). But the AL title went to Boston's Ted Williams, who batted .388.

Before Mantle burst onto the scene, switch-hitters were rare. It was unusual for a team to have more than one, and many teams had none. Then youngsters began copying Mantle's technique of batting from each side of the plate, and now we have three or four switch-hitters on a team.

After Mantle's title in '56, the league didn't have a switch-hitting leader until Willie Wilson of Kansas City hit .332 in 1982. Sixteen seasons later, switch-hitting Bernie Williams of the Yankees led the AL at .339.

In the National League, a switch-hitter has won the batting title seven times. Pete Rose was the first when he hit .335 for Cincinnati in 1968. He also won it in 1969 and 1973. Willie McGee was the champ twice (.353 in '85 and .335 in '90 with St. Louis), and Terry Pendleton (.319 in '91 with Atlanta) and Tim Raines (.334 in '86 with Montreal) also led the NL.

Remember when the Los Angeles Dodgers won the 1965 pennant with an infield of switch-hitters — Wes Parker, Jim Lefebvre, Maury Wills and Jim

Gilliam?

Ryan Lefebvre, the K.C. radio announcer, told me the ultimate switch-hitter story. His grandfather, Ben Lefebvre, who coached Sparky Anderson in high school, taught all three Lefebvre brothers to switch-hit. Jim, Ryan's dad, was the only one to reach the big leagues, but Tip and Gil played pro ball, too.

"In the mid-'80s," Ryan said, "my grandfather was closing out his 35-year coaching career. He insisted that his St. Bernard's High School team learn to switch-hit – every one of them. It wasn't easy, but they all did it. That team batted .400 for the season and won the high school championship."

Originally printed on August 22, 2001.

ERNIE HARWELL

Old ballparks live on in our memories

"There Used To Be a Ballpark Here" is a great Frank Sinatra song that suggests the yearning fans have about baseball stadiums of the past.

For example, a recent letter from Tommy W. Rogers of Jackson, Miss., asked for my recollections about Ponce de Leon Park, once home of the Atlanta Crackers of the Southern Association.

"The place now has the appearance of a dump," Mr. Rogers writes. "What should be a park, plaques, benches, regular patrols, is dangerous, forlorn, abused."

Isn't that the fate of deserted parks? Some fare a little better. Ebbets Field and the Polo Grounds have become apartment complexes, and Kansas City's Municipal Stadium is an open field. In any case, they've all been forgotten.

That brought me a flood of memories about Ponce de Leon. It was the first ballpark I ever knew. I saw my first game there on July 4, 1926, when the Crackers played the New Orleans Pelicans in a doubleheader. Later, I was the Crackers' batboy and also worked in the visitors' clubhouse.

In 1934 I covered the Crackers for the Sporting News, and when I came out of the Marines after World War II, I was their play-by-play broadcaster.

The famous magnolia on the terrace in deep centerfield was 462 feet from home. I don't think any fly ball ever reached that tree. Back of the third-base

129

stands was a public swimming pool. If the game wasn't exciting, you could enjoy some girl-watching. The park's seating capacity was 12,500. The left-field bleachers were 315 feet from home plate. And in right, three tiers of signboards reached up to the railroad tracks. Often, the train crews would stop and watch the Crackers action.

In earlier days, there were no signboards in right — just a steep embankment that presented a challenge to a rightfielder chasing a fly ball.

My top personal memories of Ponce de Leon:

The night Crackers officials, players and umpires gave special permission for my invalid dad to watch a game from our car parked in rightfield foul territory.

My return to Ponce de Leon as a Dodgers announcer in the spring of 1949. The Ku Klux Klan had threatened to kill Jackie Robinson if he played against the Crackers in the three-game exhibition series. Jackie played all three games — the first time in Atlanta history that blacks and whites had competed in a professional sports event. Each game set an attendance record. The final exhibition drew 25,221. The fans of my hometown were well-behaved.

Originally printed on May 21, 1999.

1952 Giants best proof that baseball's timeless

One of the many great attractions of baseball is that no matter how far behind a team might be, it can still win. It won't happen much, but the possibility is there. Without a clock, the losing team is never completely out of it.

I've seen great rallies and fantastic collapses. The greatest comeback or fade (depending on your loyalties) was a New York Giants-St. Louis Cardinals game June 15, 1952, at the Polo Grounds in New York.

I was broadcasting for the Giants that long, doubleheader afternoon. In the first game, the Giants scored five runs in the second inning and six in the third. After four innings, the Giants led, 11-0, with their ace, Sal Maglie, pitching. If any game ever looked like a cinch, this was it.

The Cards KO'd Maglie with a seven-run fifth. They added three runs in the seventh to make it 11-10. Solly Hemus led off the Cards' eighth with a home run and homered again in the ninth as the Cards led, 14-11. New York scored in the bottom of the ninth, but left the bases loaded.

The Giants had blown an 11-0 lead. With the big lead, manager Leo Durocher made a fatal mistake and pulled some veterans from the lineup. Slugging outfielder Bob Elliott and veteran catcher Wes Westrum were rested so they would be ready for the second game.

The Cardinals' manager was Durocher's protege, Eddie Stanky. He didn't make the same mistake.

"Something told me not to make any changes," Stanky recalled. "I'm glad I didn't because the players I would have removed (Stan Musial, Red Schoendienst and Enos Slaughter) stayed in there and helped us come from behind to win that game. Once we had the momentum and got rid of Maglie, everything went our way. It was a sweet win for us."

I don't remember the second game of that doubleheader. But I'll never forget the first. It brought home to me the lesson that a baseball game is never over until the last batter is out.

And that's one of the many reasons baseball is such a great game.

Originally printed on September 14, 1996.

Misunderstood stars always special to me

It's difficult to explain, but I've always had an affinity for the mavericks of baseball. I'm referring to the so-called misunderstood — the guys who can't get along with the media. Most earn appreciation — and sometimes affection — from teammates. Others aren't ever accepted by those who play, travel and live with them.

The first of them I knew well was Jim Rivera. I met him when he was in the Atlanta Federal Penitentiary (I was just visiting, thank you), long before he became a star outfielder with the Browns and White Sox. While with Chicago, he visited my Baltimore home for lunch. Lulu had prepared a wonderful meal: salad, soup, steak and vegetables. Jim asked her, "Lulu, do you serve this slop to everybody?" She understood Jim and his ways and took his remark with good humor.

Some other misunderstood players I liked were Alex Johnson, the Detroiter who became an American League batting champion with the Angels in 1970 before finishing his career with the Tigers in 1976; Eddie Murray, the new Hall of Famer; and Silent George Hendrick, who after hitting three home runs in a 1973 game for Cleveland against the Tigers, decided never to speak to the media again.

Then there was Dick Allen, one of the best hitters I ever saw. When he was with the White Sox, Dick was his own man. Manager Chuck Tanner allowed Allen a separate set of rules. Allen often reported late and sometimes missed batting practice. I was waiting to interview him when he arrived late at Tiger Stadium. I sat next to him and started my tape machine. After a brief introduction, he shouted to a batboy, "Have you seen my sweatshirt? Where's my shirt?" I kept the tape rolling, then I said, "Dick, you've just come over from the National League. Who are some of the pitchers in the American League who have been tough for you to hit?"

"I don't think I can answer that," he said. "If you'd ask me about National League pitchers, I could tell you."

"OK," I said, "Who are the tough pitchers in the National League?"

"I don't think I can answer that," he said.

Next is Barry Bonds, a prime example of the misunderstood star. I don't know Bonds or the demons he has battled, but I do know he's one of the top three players ever. I certainly admire him for that.

My heart goes out to him. His father, Bobby, died Saturday, after suffering lung cancer, a brain tumor and heart trouble. Barry had left the Giants for several games to be at Bobby's bedside. Yet, when he did play, he was still the ferocious, dominating slugger. The only time he could relax and get away from the tragic reality of his father's illness was when he was playing his nine innings.

Barry Bonds, the player, might be one of those who is misunderstood. But all of us can understand Barry Bonds, the son of a dying father.

Originally printed on August 25, 2003.

Always keep
'em laughing

Good-natured insults bejewel diamond game

When they played for the St. Louis Cardinals, first baseman Bill White and pitcher Bob Gibson were close friends. One of their strongest bonds was a determination to win. One night Gibson found himself in a horrendous pitching jam. White came over from first base to encourage him. Even before Bill reached the mound, Gibson stared him down with his famous scowl.

"What are you doing here?" he grunted. "The only thing you know about pitching is that you can't hit it."

It was an example of the many put-downs that happen in baseball — even between the best of friends.

The 1968 Tigers gave us a dandy. Weak-hitting Ray Oyler (he batted .135 that season) was at the plate with two out. The next hitter was Dick McAuliffe. When Dick came to the on-deck circle, he didn't bring a bat. Instead, he knelt there with a glove.

One of my favorite baseball personalities was the big, intimidating pitcher Goose Gossage. When he entered a game, he was so menacing that hitters wanted to hide in the dugout. But one night at Yankee Stadium, outfielder Mickey Rivers, a character in his own right, turned the tables on Gossage, his fellow Yankee.

For the past several outings, Gossage had run into trouble and was in a rut, struggling to get anybody out. When the Goose came in from the bullpen, Rivers was in centerfield. Rivers then turned his back to the diamond and assumed the hands-on-the-ground stance of a sprinter, ready to race after any long fly ball hit over his head.

I was the victim of a put-down by the master of the art — Norman Cash. Norman gave me an autographed photo of himself. On the picture he wrote, "To my good friend, Ernie Harwell, the second-best announcer in the big leagues. The other 25 tied for first place."

That one was good-natured and from a great guy. I'm not too sure about the put-down that Tommy Lasorda, then manager of the Dodgers, directed at his rightfielder, Darryl Strawberry. Here is the quote from Tommy: "No, I wouldn't ever call Strawberry a dog. After all, a dog is loyal and will chase after a ball."

Originally printed on May 10, 2002.

Sparky just managed to slide by

Our newest Hall of Famer, Sparky Anderson, has been inundated with glowing words. He can gracefully accept those compliments. He also knows how to take a few friendly jibes. Here is a banquet skit I aimed at the Spark in January 1983:

This is a Tigers low-light presentation — not a motion picture. The Tigers haven't been in motion since 1972. ... It's a slide presentation. Nothing new, the Tigers have been on a slide for the past 10 years. ...

So let's look at our slides.

- **First slide:** June 1979, Kalamazoo. ... John Fetzer thinking about firing Les Moss as Tigers manager. ... Fetzer is reading his copy of Rolling Stone — gathering no Moss.

- **Next slide:** Fetzer, humming "I need a gal in Kalamazoo" ... phones Jim Campbell. Fetzer says, "Jim, fire Moss. ... Get that Loni Anderson from Cincinnati. If Moss can't win with Dan Gonzales, Ed Putman, Dave Machemer and Sheldon Burnside, he can't win with anybody. ... I want to see Les of Moss and more of Loni."

- **Next slide:** An excited Campbell is phoning Sparky Anderson, too excited to realize Fetzer wanted Loni Anderson.

- **Next slide:** Background on Sparky. ... Real name: George. Little George, 6 years old, is being vaccinated for school. They're using what was then called a Victrola needle.

138

- **Next slide:** George's mother talking: "All you want to do, George, is play baseball. How will you ever make it in this cruel world?" George answers: "I'll manage."
- **Next slide:** George attending Casey Stengel University of the King's English. ... The Dean (Dizzy Dean) is talking: "George, I want you to major in the care and treatment of language fractures. ... Think you can handle it?" George says: "I'll manage."
- **Next slide:** 1959 ... Sparky now playing with the Phillies. ... His manager, Eddie Sawyer, says: "George, how you gonna stay in baseball? There's no place for a .218 hitter." George says, "I'll manage."
- **Next slide:** Sparky at Cincinnati. ... He's won only four National League pennants, but the GM, Dick Wagner, is writing his own Wagnerian opera. ...So Sparky comes to Detroit. ... Fetzer thought he was getting Loni Anderson. Jim Campbell settled for Sparky Anderson. ... And a lot of the fans and media who have heard Sparky's fairy tales are beginning to believe the Tigers got Hans Christian Andersen!
- **Next slide:** Spring training 1983. ... Sparky's office in Lakeland. ... Tom Gage, Brian Bragg, Vern Plagenhoef — the beat writers — are with Sparky. Sparky says: "You guys aren't qualified to write baseball. How do you think you can cover my team for a whole season?" They all answer in unison: "We'll manage."
- **Final slide:** Sparky on phone with Campbell. ...He says: "These writers think they can manage my

club. ... What shall I do?" Campbell says: "Go to the bar. ... Buy them all Sparky Anderson cocktails. ... They'll never bother you again." Sparky says: "What's a Sparky Anderson cocktail?" Jim answers: "A Sparky Anderson cocktail? Three of them, and you can't manage anything all summer long."

Originally printed on April 28, 2000.

Bottom of the ninth was never funnier

I t used to be that we heard most of our jokes at the barbershop, the office or a bar. Not anymore. Now people spend their waking hours sending jokes over the Internet.

When I'm online, I try to ignore most of these attempts at humor. But once in a while, one comes along that hits me on the funny bone. Here's one that combines two of my chief interests — baseball and music. I don't know who wrote this joke, how it got started, or who put it on the Internet. But, here it is:

The city's symphony orchestra was performing Beethoven's Ninth. This symphony has a passage of about 20 minutes when the bass violinists have nothing to do.

Rather than just sit around while others played, some bassists decided to sneak to the tavern next door for some strengthening refreshments. After slamming down several whiskeys in quick succession, one looked at his watch and said, "Hey, guys, it's time. We better get back on stage."

"No need to panic, my friend," a fellow bassist said. "I figured we might need a little more time, so I tied the last few pages of the conductor's score together with string. You can be sure it will take him at least a few minutes to get it all untangled."

Several drinks later, they staggered back to the concert hall and, very carefully, took their places on stage. One of the newspaper critics in the audience took a close look at the conductor and noticed a change in his demeanor.

He turned to his companion and said: "The conductor looks upset and nervous. He seems to me to be a bit edgy." His companion didn't seem surprised.

"Why, of course," he said. "Don't you see? It's the bottom of the Ninth, the score is tied, and the bassists are loaded."

Please don't blame me for that one. I simply found it on the Internet and thought I would pass it along.

Originally printed on August 18, 2000.

ERNIE HARWELL

Restaurateur got last laugh at funeral

To say funerals aren't much fun is the ultimate understatement.

This is a story about how a deceased brought a smile and a chuckle to those around the grave site — even after his casket had been lowered into the ground. The story comes from one of the pallbearers, John Ginopolis, a Farmington Hills restaurateur.

John's uncle, Ted Gregory, owned a famous Montgomery Inn restaurant in Cincinnati. He had been in business for more than 50 years, building a worldwide reputation for ribs. He shipped ribs to sheiks in Saudi Arabia, to monarchs of Europe, and to movie stars in Hollywood or on location around the world.

Ted knew everybody — actors, media moguls, politicians and athletes. He was a man-about-town, a bon vivant and a practical joker. Nobody loved a practical joke as much as Ted Gregory.

When Gregory died in December 2001, his funeral attracted more than 3,000 of his closest friends. They came from everywhere and packed the church. Because the crowd was so large, the Cincinnati police were forced to close two highway exits and divert traffic.

After the church service, the funeral procession proceeded slowly to the cemetery. Solemn-faced admirers gathered graveside for their final look at Ted, their longtime friend. Eyes teared and hand-

143

kerchiefs were pulled from purses and pockets. The casket was lowered into the ground, and the funeral was over.

No, wait a minute. The, ceremony wasn't over after all. The funeral director approached the pall-bearers.

"Gentlemen," he said, "Mr. Gregory's final wish was that each of you smoke a cigar here after he was lowered into the grave."

Then the funeral director handed cigars to the six pallbearers. They lit their cigars. BAM! Each cigar exploded.

Next, the funeral director gave the startled pall-bearers a note.

They read their notes, and a smile broke out on all six faces. The note said: "Always keep 'em laughing." Signed: Ted Gregory.

Yes, even from the grave, Ted Gregory remained a practical joker.

Originally printed on September 16, 2003.

ERNIE HARWELL

Cookies can land a man or a fortune

Bake cookies.
That's my advice to young ladies who want to land a rich husband or start a successful business.

Cookies have been the secret of success for at least two baseball ladies. First, there's the story of Anne Mellqueham, who became the wife of Mike Scioscia, manager of the World Series champion Anaheim Angels. This story emerged from a Scioscia profile that Diane Pucin wrote in the Los Angeles Times magazine.

Anne attended autograph day at Dodger Stadium with a plate of cookies she had baked especially for Mike. But because of other duties in the clubhouse, Scioscia did not appear as scheduled. There stood Anne with her plate of culinary handiwork and nowhere to go. She felt embarrassed and frustrated. A sympathetic security guard tried to help.

"He gave me his name and told me to meet him at the Dodger clubhouse after the game," Anne said. "Then he introduced me to Mike. I gave Mike the cookies. He immediately bit into one and smiled."

The next thing Anne knew, Scioscia was walking her to his car in the players' parking lot. That was the beginning. They dated for five years and then got married — a union that has lasted 17 years.

The other lady famous for cookies is Debbie Fields. Mrs. Fields' Original Cookies have more that 650 domestic locations and more than 655 interna-

145

tional stores in 11 countries. But not too many years ago, she — like Anne Scioscia — was a young lady bringing cookies to the ballpark.

In the early '70s Debbie was a ballgirl for the Athletics at the Oakland Coliseum. She began to bake cookies and take them to the players. They loved them. Some players suggested she go into the business of baking and selling cookies and even agreed to back her financially. She opened her first store in Palo Alto, Calif., in August 1977.

Debbie Fields is now a worldwide celebrity and has developed her company into a premier chain of cookie and baked goods stores.

Yes, ladies, if you want a famous husband 'or a thriving business enterprise, I advise you: Bake cookies.

Originally printed on June 18, 2003.

Stallings: Dead man walking

Baseball's saddest refrain is "Oh, those bases on balls."

It's a mournful phrase uttered by most any manager during most any game — a phrase echoing through decades of diamond history. Nobody knows who said it first, but we all have heard it time and again.

In the late 1940s the phrase became a signature for New York Giants broadcaster Frankie Frisch. But his distaste for walks stemmed from his experience as manager for the Cards, Pirates and Cubs. When I tuned in, Frisch's hatred of the walk burned deepest into my brain.

But Frisch's tirade pales in comparison to the feelings expressed so often by George Stallings. A colorful character with a long career in baseball, he was the Tigers' first manager, but won most of his fame by leading the Boston Braves of 1914 to a miracle comeback. Coming from last place on July 4 (11½ games back), the Braves won the National League pennant and then swept Connie Mack's highly favored Athletics in the World Series.

Stallings was sadistic, sarcastic and profane. He was never more revealing of those qualities than when provoked by a walk thrown by one of his pitchers. Stallings' third baseman, Carlisle (Red) Smith, was an Atlantan and a good friend of mine when I started writing for the Sporting News in the mid-1930s. Smith told me many stories about Stallings.

The shortstop on that same Stallings team was Hall of Famer Rabbit Maranville.

I knew Rabbit long after he had retired and was working for Hearst newspapers in New York as director of their sandlot baseball program.

Rabbit told the story — probably apocryphal — that epitomizes Stalling's deep hatred for bases on balls.

Here's the way Maranville related the story:

In 1929, Stallings became ill in Montreal. He went from specialist to specialist, but doctors could find neither the cure nor the cause of his illness. His wife decided to take him back home to Haddock, Ga. During the trip by ambulance from Atlanta to Haddock, Stallings fell into a deep coma. The doctor in the ambulance asked Mrs. Stallings, "What caused the trouble?"

"Nobody knows," she answered. "We had all the specialists in Canada treat George, but not one of them could find the cause."

At that moment Stallings came out of his coma. He raised himself up and shouted at the doctor, "Bases on balls, you fathead. That was the cause of it all."

Then he fell back and died.

Oh, those bases on balls.

Originally printed on May 2, 2003.

ERNIE HARWELL

Banter in the words of the bard

couple of years ago, a reader sent me biblical answers to some baseball questions. As a follow-up, here is a set of questions answered with quotes from Shakespeare.

This all started when Barry Wood of the Voice of America interviewed me on television last summer in Baltimore. Afterward, he sent me a book, "Shakespeare on Baseball," compiled by David Goodnough. The questions are mine. The answers are from Gentle Will via Mr. Goodnough.

- What did the pitcher say when he gave up two successive dinky Texas Leaguers? "Why is not this a lamentable thing, that we should be thus afflicted with these strange flies?" — "Romeo and Juliet."
- What was the baserunner's reaction when he was flashed the steal sign? "By heaven, I'll steal away." — "All's Well That Ends Well."
- What did the team's top slugger say to himself after he had worked his favorite pitcher to a 3-0 count? "My Lord, I'll hit him now." — "Hamlet."
- What did the superstar tell his agent about endorsements? "Make my image but an alehouse sign." — "King Henry VI."
- How did the owner characterize the beat writers? "Poor berating orators of miseries, let them have scope." — "King Richard III."
- What was the manager's instruction to his weakest hitter? "O, let me see thee walk." — "The Taming of the Shrew."

149

- What did the hitting coach say about extra batting practice? "To business that we love we rise betime, and go to't with delight." — "Antony and Cleopatra."
- What was the angry manager's criticism of his many overanxious hitters? "How poor they are that have no patience." — "Othello."
- How did the fans describe the graceful shortstop? "Custom hath made it in him a property of easiness." — "Hamlet."
- What was the umpire's answer to the angry manager? "If you have any pity, grace or manners, you would not make me such an argument." — "A Midsummer Night's Dream."
- How did the sports writer describe the injury-prone star? "Like a strutting player, whose conceit lies in his hamstring, and doth think it rich to hear the wooden dialogue and sound 'twixt his stretched footage and the scaffoldage." — "Troilus and Cressida."
- What can we learn from the out-of-town scoreboard? "Who loses and who wins, who's in, who's out." — "King Lear."
- What is the pitcher's game plan? "To mow 'em down before me." — "King Henry VIII."
- How do players feel about some fans? "How earnestly they knock!" — "Troilus and Cressida."
- What did the umpire say to calm the two protesting managers? "Seal up the mouth of outrage for a while, till we can clear these ambiguities." — "Romeo and Juliet."

Originally printed on July 27, 2001.

Closer

Oh, those sportscasters: Talk about strange

Asportscaster is a strange creature. From 200 feet, he can identify the pitch as a slider on the outside corner, but he can't tell you the color of his wife's eyes.

He can paint a glowing word picture of the San Gabriel mountains past the rim of the Rose Bowl, but when he goes to the hardware store, he is always asking for one of those thingamabobs that will fit into a whatchamacallit.

He's a reporter, entertainer, salesman, teacher, orator and philosopher. Others would murder to get a ticket to the game, but the sportscaster gets in free and has the best seat in the stadium. And every fan knows that broadcasting a game is the easiest job in the world.

As a kid third baseman, the sportscaster couldn't stop a grapefruit from rolling uphill, but he can tell three million listeners that Cal Ripken should have played that last hitter at least five steps to the left.

He gets letters, too, and some are very kind. The others, he turns over to the FBI. One lady writes: "I want you to go away with me."

He remembers his first date with his wife — easy, it was the night of the first Ali/Frazier fight. And he can memorize the uniform numbers of 55 players on a college football team, but he can't recall which dry cleaners has his shirts.

A sportscaster likes action-packed games, hot coffee, big, excited crowds, friendly press rooms, loyal fans and free food and drink. He dislikes dou-bleheaders, freezing football weather, rain delays and mumbling athletes who punctuate every sen-tence with "you know, you know."

He dresses like Woody Allen, jokes like Tim Allen, and his wife looks like Steve Allen.

He can smooth-talk a worldwide Super Bowl audience, but he's tongue-tied at the PTA meeting.

His fans love him, athletes tolerate him, and his family calls him Daddy.

Looking back, he realizes it has been a good life.

He has seen the stars in action.

From Jimmy Brown to Reggie Jackson,

Elvin Hayes and Willie Mays,

Roger Maris and Bucky Harris,

As he narrates their parade,

Wondering if it's just charade.

He can be vindictive or forgiving.

For all the games that he saw played,

Remember, now, he never paid.

Beats working for a living.

Originally printed on September 27, 1997.

Good-bye, and thank you

Stories and photos from Harwell's farewell

Ernie says 'good-bye' and 'hello'

Ernie Harwell's final address from his last Tigers broadcast, Sunday, Sept. 29, 2002

"The Tigers have just finished their 2002 season. And I've just finished my baseball broadcasting career, and it's time to say good-bye. But I think good-byes are sad, and I'd much rather say hello. Hello to a new adventure.

"I'm not leaving, folks. I'll still be with you, living my life in Michigan, my home state, surrounded by family and friends.

"And rather than good-bye, please allow me to say thank you.

"Thank you for letting me be part of your family. Thank you for taking me with you to that cottage Up North, to the beach, the picnic, your workplace and your backyard.

"Thank you for sneaking your transistor under the pillow as you grew up loving the Tigers.

"Now I might have been a small part of your life. But you have been a very large part of mine. And it's my privilege and honor to share with you the greatest game of all.

"Now God has a new adventure for me. And I'm ready to move on. So I leave you with a deep sense of appreciation for your longtime loyalty and support.

"I thank you very much, and God bless all of you."

JULIAN H. GONZALEZ/Detroit Free Press

Ernie Harwell waves to the crowd during the seventh-inning stretch at Comerica Park on Sept. 22, 2002 – the last home game of his career as the Tigers' broadcaster.

CHIP SOMODEVILLA/Detroit Free Press

Ernie is cheered by fans as he heads off the field and through the tunnel after a ceremony in his honor on Sept. 15, 2002 – Ernie Harwell Day – at Comerica Park.

ERIC SEALS/Detroit Free Press

Bob Pachella of Ann Arbor waits with a baseball for Ernie Harwell to autograph before a 2002 spring game at Lakeland, Fla.

HUGH GRANNUM/Detroit Free Press

Ernie and Lulu Harwell relax in the summer of 2003 at their Michigan home. "Lulu and I have traveled a lot, so we might just take it easy for a little while," Ernie said in 2002 of his looming retirement.

158

ERIC SEALS/Detroit Free Press

**Ernie Harwell fills out the lineup on his scorecard before the Tigers'
spring opener versus Pittsburgh on Feb. 28, 2002, at Lakeland, Fla.**

Signing off: Reflecting on his legend, legacy and life

By MIKE BRUDENELL
Free Press Sports Writer

Ernie Harwell would like his legacy and life after baseball kept neat and simple.

Harwell, 84, will retire as the voice of the Tigers after the season's last game, Sept. 29 at Toronto. The Tigers will honor him Sept. 15 with Ernie Harwell Day at Comerica Park, and his final home game will be Sept. 22, when the Tigers play the Yankees.

Harwell isn't much for fancy trimmings. He would prefer no tributes, although he knows he probably will get them. He hasn't planned any lengthy trips, either, although he might one day go on another cruise with his wife, Lulu, whom he married in 1941.

"I'd like to be remembered as someone who showed up for the job," Harwell said this week. "I consider myself a worker. I love what I do. If I had my time over again, I'd probably do it for nothing."

As far as vacations go, Harwell thinks "tooling around" in northern Michigan during fall would be just fine for now.

Harwell, who has spent 55 years broadcasting in the major leagues, joined the Tigers as a play-by-play announcer in 1960. His partner at the time was former Tigers third baseman George Kell.

"I had a job to do, and I did it all these years to the best of my ability," Harwell said. "That's what I'd like to leave behind as I finish my final game in Toronto."

For thousands of Detroit fans, Harwell's last day behind the microphone will stir emotions and evoke memories of simpler times, when the game seemed to make more sense.

But Harwell, who would rather look ahead than behind, thinks the game is in capable hands, in the booth and on the diamond.

"Someone much better at this than me will come along soon," said Harwell, inducted into the Baseball Hall of Fame in 1981. "They always do. The fans will shower him or her with affection."

Despite the recent threat of a baseball strike, Harwell thinks the game is too good to disappear or self-destruct.

"I love the game because it's so simple, yet it can be so complex," Harwell said. "There's a lot of layers to it, but they aren't hard to peel back.

"Baseball has been handed down from father to son, from generation to generation. I don't expect that to change."

Harwell admits baseball has taken a few u-turns through the years but isn't too worried about its future.

"I think it's on the right track," he said. "The game goes in cycles, and it's been slow to change compared to some sports. But that's not all bad."

Baseball's tradition, Harwell said, will keep it strong.

"If I walked back into the booth in the year 2025, I don't think it would have changed much," he said. "I think baseball would be played and managed pretty much the same as it is today. It's a great survivor."

Would he want a part of it again?

"I think so," he said.

Harwell, born Jan. 25, 1918, at Washington, Ga., began covering the Atlanta Crackers minor league baseball team as a reporter for the Sporting News in the mid-1930s. After he became a broadcaster in Atlanta, he was hired by the Brooklyn Dodgers in 1948, the year after Jackie Robinson crossed baseball's color line. Harwell later worked for the New York Giants (1950-53) and Baltimore Orioles (1954-59).

"I followed my dreams as a young man," Harwell said. "With Miss Lulu's support, I'd do it all again. I couldn't have done it without her. We've had a great adventure. God has been good to us."

Harwell includes watching Willie Mays make his debut with the Giants in 1951 and Bobby Thomson's historic home run off Ralph Branca in the 1951 National League playoffs as two moments he always will cherish.

"Mays was simply the best," Harwell said. "He could throw, hit and run.

"And I thought the Dodgers were home against the Giants. Then Thompson unloads against Branca. You can never be sure in baseball."

The friendships made with players and fellow broadcasters, Harwell said, will serve him well into his retirement.

"I hate to single out players and journalists, because I've met so many good people throughout my career," said Harwell, who lives in Lakeland, Fla., three months a year and will continue to divide his time between Michigan and Florida. "But I can say

I've always enjoyed my days with Al Kaline. I also thought Frank Tanana was a fun guy to be around.

"As far as broadcasters go, my time with Paul Carey in Detroit was special. We worked together from 1973-91. Paul worked hard, and he was very loyal to me."

While one adventure draws to a close for Harwell, another chapter of his life begins.

"I've got a lot of books to read and plays to see," said Harwell, who also might return to writing songs, which he has done in the past for artists such as Mitch Ryder and B.J. Thomas. "Lulu and I have traveled a lot, so we might just take it easy for a little while. After all, we do have the best bed and food right at home.

"But we'll certainly go south to see family and friends whenever we can. I'd also like to watch as many baseball games as possible on TV or listen to them on radio."

After seven decades covering baseball, Harwell is ready to move on.

"Baseball is a lot like life," he said. "It's a day-to-day existence, full of ups and downs. You make the most of your opportunities in baseball as you do in life.

"I'm not going to waste a day after I call my last play."

Originally printed on Sept. 13, 2002

KIRTHMON F. DOZIER/Detroit Free Press

Ernie Harwell embraces his wife, Lulu, whom he wed in 1941. "I followed my dreams as a young man," he said. "With Miss Lulu's support, I'd do it all again. I couldn't have done it without her. We've had a great adventure. God has been good to us."

Harwell salutes fans as a large part of his life

By JOHN LOWE
Free Press Sports Writer

TORONTO — Ernie Harwell felt emotion overtake him once Sunday during his final Tigers broadcast. It happened a few moments after the game, when he read his farewell address.

Holding his printed copy of the address, he pointed to the line where he almost couldn't keep going. "It was down here," he said, "where I said, 'I might have been a small part of your life, but you've been a large part of mine.'

"I felt almost teary, almost choking. I began to say to myself, 'Am I going to get through it or not?'"

He said those emotions welled in him because "I felt so much affection for the fans. I don't think it had to do with my leaving. My appreciation for what people have done for me is so deep and so true."

Despite that flood of feelings, the man who in his 55-season major league career missed two games — neither because of faulty health — kept the words coming.

In the one-minute, 15-second farewell address, and as usual during the game, Harwell used the spare and sturdy style he learned as a newspaperman from his Atlanta Constitution sports editor, Ralph McGill, more than 60 years ago.

"Two down, a man on, Mr. Escobar trying to get that final out," he said, enthusiastically anticipating

KIRTHMON F. DOZIER/Detroit Free Press

Ernie Harwell contemplates a Tiger jersey presented during a tribute
to him at Comerica Park. Harwell was the voice of the Tigers from
1960 to 2002.

JULIAN H. GONZALEZ/Detroit Free Press

Ernie flips his hat to the crowd from the broadcast booth at Comerica
Park during his final home game as the Tigers' radio voice – on
Sept. 22, 2002.

the game's climax. "Pena digging in, waiting. Here's the set, the pitch. Swing and a miss, and the Toronto Blue Jays win the final game of 2002. The final score, the Blue Jays one and the Tigers nothing."

Break to commercial.

The time was 3:18 p.m.

It had been one more classic Harwell broadcast. He regularly gave the score, and he unfurled stories and similes you won't hear from anyone else.

"We had a team in Baltimore that had such bad hitters they called them a 'Kleenex Team,'" he said in the third inning. "They popped up one at a time."

In the seventh, he said, "One of my large regrets is that I never got to Cuba. The Dodgers trained in Cuba one year. Hugh Casey got in a fight with Ernest Hemingway."

With the score 0-0 in the bottom of the eighth, Harwell said, "Like the fat lady's girdle, something's got to break loose."

He needed only 12 syllables to describe Eric Hinske's winning hit: "a little, slow, lazy line drive over third base."

When Eric Munson repeatedly fouled pitches en route to a two-out walk in the ninth, Harwell, in a rare moment of self-perspective, said, "Fifty-five years of ball one/strike one — I guess I can wait for another couple of pitches."

The last words he spoke on the air were the final words of his farewell address: "Thank you very much, and God bless you."

Moments later, he said of the farewell, "I wanted it to be as natural as it could be. I didn't want to get too literary, or too poetic, or too fancy or too contrived."

Harwell, 84, has spent half his life as a Tigers announcer, mostly as the lead radio broadcaster. He decided last winter he would retire after this season, and he felt at peace with the decision as Sunday neared.

From the moment he arrived Sunday at the SkyDome until the final out, he was as relaxed and sunny as ever. He never cried and never got the chills.

As soon as the commercial break began after the final out, Harwell — fully alive with the game — told his colleagues in the booth, "Hey, hey, hey," in the joyous crescendo of someone who had just broadcast his first game.

Harwell is one of the last direct links to what he calls "the early days of baseball."

As a sports announcer in his early 20s at Atlanta radio station WSB, Harwell in the early 1940s interviewed Connie Mack, the Philadelphia Athletics' patriarchal manager. Mack, born when Lincoln was president, became the Athletics' manager in 1901, the first year of the American League and of the game's modern history. By virtue of eventually becoming the club owner, Mack held the job through 1950, Harwell's third season in the majors.

Next season — for the first time in the 103-year modern history of baseball — neither Mack nor Harwell will be in the big leagues.

Instead, Harwell will continue to do commercials, write a Free Press column and do vignettes for Fox Sports Net, and perhaps write his fifth book.

After his farewell address Sunday, he did a TV

KIRTHMON F. DOZIE/Detroit Free Press

Of his 55 years broadcasting major league baseball, Ernie Harwell said: "I'd like to be remembered as someone who showed up for the job. I consider myself a worker. I love what I do. If I had my time over again, I'd probably do it for nothing.

KIRTHMON F. DOZIER/Detroit Free Press

Lulu Harwell waves to fans celebrating Ernie Harwell Day at Comerica Park. After Ernie's 55 years of broadcasting, the Harwells learned there is life after baseball.

interview with Fox Sports Net's Mario Impemba and Kirk Gibson, who had a tear down his cheek. Then Harwell, who said Sunday that "I got into radio by mistake," went to the dugout to discuss his day with the people whose profession he once aspired to, the sports writers.

"I didn't feel nervous at all," he told them. "I had a peace and a quiet that God has given me. I knew I was going to be relaxed and have a real good time. . . . I feel great. My main feeling is one of relief. It's like high school graduation. It's over. I can go to the prom now. . . . I look on life as a joyous adventure, and whatever is coming next, I'm ready for."

He next went to the Tigers' clubhouse to wish the best to the more than 20 players he saw and to manager Luis Pujols.

Then he went back up to the broadcast booth to pack up his pens, notes and scorecard, which looks just like the one he used for the most thrilling moment of his career, Bobby Thomson's pennant-winning homer for the New York Giants in 1951.

At 4:11 p.m., he walked out of a broadcast booth for the last time as a major league announcer.

His prodigious resume had one noticeable blank.

He never broadcast a perfect game.

But he broadcast thousands of games perfectly.

Free Press special writer David Enders contributed.

Originally printed on Sept. 30, 2002

CHIP SOMODEVILLA/Detroit Free Press

Ernie Harwell gives a thumbs-up to fans at Comerica Park on Ernie Harwell Day. "I feel great," he said after his final broadcast Sept. 29, 2002. "I look on life as a joyous adventure, and whatever is coming next, I'm ready for."

Paying Tribute

AL broadcasters on Harwell's legacy

AL broadcasters on Harwell and his legacy

No one recognizes a professional's skill and value like his or her peers. Throughout Ernie Harwell's final season, Free Press sports writer John Lowe talked to Harwell's fellow American League broadcasters about him.

What emerged is a dual tribute to Harwell: recognition that he has made a lasting contribution to the standard for excellence in baseball broadcasting, and appreciation of what a warm friend and colleague he has been.

With a handful of exceptions, all of the broadcasters to whom we talked are, like Harwell, full-time radio announcers. Frank Beckmann, the Tigers' play-by-play announcer on Channel 50, served as the Tigers' radio voice in 1995-98, part of his continuing career of high quality and immense versatility on Detroit radio. Seattle's Dave Niehaus, who divides his time between radio and television, remains at heart a radio man. Rick Rizzs, Niehaus' TV and radio colleague with the Mariners, won the honor in 1992 of succeeding Harwell as the Tigers' lead radio announcer. And Josh Lewin, the play-by-play announcer for Texas telecasts, studied Harwell's broadcasts as he grew up, then became his Detroit colleague.

Here is what these voices of the game have to say about Harwell:

Ernie always knew game's tempo

Bill King, Oakland Athletics

When you hear Ernie Harwell's honey tones, and that wonderful timbre of the voice and the cadence, if it's in the background and you don't even hear the distinct words and phrases, it says to you, "That's baseball." I think that is one of the things that certain broadcasters have.

Vin Scully has that same quality. If you were to listen to Vin and hear his voice in the distance, you'd know, "That's baseball." That's summer. That's a warm evening, a hot afternoon. And that's baseball to me, because I go back to the time prior to television as a kid growing up, there was that sound on radio.

Coming from radio myself — a child of radio — I think I have a greater appreciation of Ernie than people of a younger generation. They appreciate Ernie, but maybe not for the same reasons that I do.

Baseball is the sport most suited to radio. It's the theatre of the mind.

The challenge of the broadcaster is to bring to the fans the total picture, the interpretation of the game, be the eyes and ears of fans. Ernie does it so well. You can do it in a complex fashion that you set the listener spinning. Ernie keeps it simple and yet comprehensive.

Ernie has such a wonderful voice and tempo for baseball, and it reflects the tempo of the game, which is unique.

Then of course you take it further because Ernie has such an incisive understanding of the game, such great recollections, so many years and events and experiences to draw upon to weave the tale of the game.

Baseball isn't just the balls and the strikes and the two-out hit to right-centerfield that ties the game. Baseball is a tapestry woven verbally to the listener that ties 1910 to 1990, and 2002 back to 1952.

There always seems to be a way to tie in the game to its history and its roots. And nobody does that better than Ernie.

It's been even more satisfying to get to know Ernie, after having heard him many years before I first met him, to find out not only is he such an affable and interesting man, but a very total person, and a guy who has a great consideration for his fellow man and an appreciation for many other areas of life other than just baseball and broadcasting.

That makes a total package.

Best mentor for young broadcasters
Joe Castiglione, Boston Red Sox

He's been a mentor over the years in many ways, personally and professionally, both for myself and for my family. In my first year with the Red Sox, I was getting critiqued rather harshly by one of the Boston papers. Ernie said, "You're the new guy, withstand it, and persevere and go from there."

My son had a similar situation. He met Ernie once when he came with me to Tiger Stadium. Later, my son got a job in New York as a sports anchor, and the night before he went on, he was almost physically ill, he was so nervous. He called Ernie, and Ernie said, "Look, we all go through that; you'll be fine." He felt a lot better about the situation.

One thing I've learned from Ernie is to help young broadcasters. There's never been a better guy at helping young broadcasters. He knows everybody's name. He remembers them. Ernie set an example about helping these young broadcasters.

Another big thing I've learned from Ernie is to stay contemporary. Ernie is the most contemporary octogenarian I've ever known. He stays young, he thinks young. He doesn't live in the past, which is remarkable. I asked him the other day, "Are the broadcasters today as good as they were then?"He said, "They're probably better. They're more conscientious, they work harder, they're better prepared."I thought that was reassuring from someone who has been around 60 years.

I think there's also a spirituality factor with Ernie. He lives his faith. It helps him. He is so stress-free.

Welcome to the major leagues
Paul Olden, Tampa Bay Devil Rays

When I first made it to the major leagues in 1988 with Cleveland, I packed up and went to spring training. I walked into the public relations office to introduce myself, and they said, "Oh, here's a letter for you." I thought, "Who knows I am here?"

I opened it, and it was a welcome-to-the-major-leagues note from Ernie. He had no idea who I was, but obviously he wanted to welcome to the big leagues a new kid in the fraternity.

Ernie's a friend and mentor

Josh Lewin, Texas Rangers

I grew up trying to pull in as many radio stations as I could, listening to as many guys as I could. But I always found myself on WJR, almost like it was a magnet, because of Ernie. He was such a welcoming voice. I felt like I already knew him even before I had the pleasure of meeting him. He has that effect on a lot of listeners — he's the next-door-neighbor type.

When I came to Detroit, he was the first one to reach out his hand. In my first spring training, he called to ask when I was getting in. I checked in to the hotel, and I'm there for 10 minutes just unpacking and my phone rings and it's Ernie inviting me over for dinner. So I stopped and picked up fresh strawberries for him and Miss Lulu. I thought I would just put in an appearance. He had me over for like five hours. I thought, "I guess I'm in the Tigers family now." I'll never forget that.

Ernie has turned out to be a remarkable friend — not just a mentor, but a friend. He transcends age and pretty much everything else. We don't have very much in common other than that we're very passionate about baseball and describing it to other people.

He's a master craftsman. He's always kept it simple, which I think is part of his charm and staying power.

Ernie told you what you needed to know, he told you what you didn't know, and he always had that warmth, that inviting lilt to his voice that always made you feel welcome. No one can do that like

Ernie can.

The Tigers haven't been a good team for a long time. You never ever would think "bitter old man" with Ernie. I think a lot of guys, when they start advancing into their senior years, in general become curmudgeonly. Ernie is still so high on life, and that's what plays so well in his broadcast. It's not affected, it's not an act. It's very, very genuine. I think it's remarkable.

First of all, most people his age aren't doing nearly what he's doing in terms of travel and day-to-day work. But to keep such a sunny disposition, even when the team is 15 or 30 games under .500, is just remarkable to me. He will be sorely, sorely missed, not just by me but by every other broadcaster in the business.

I think he's going to live to 112, and could have kept broadcasting until he was 102. But I totally respect that he feels it's time. It's a bummer for the rest of us.

ERNIE HARWELL

Ernie gave grand advice
Ed Farmer, Chicago White Sox

When I first started broadcasting, Ernie said, "Edward, be yourself. Just be yourself. That's all I'm going to tell you. People will like your voice, because you have a nice, pleasant tone. Tell them where the ball is. They just want to know where the ball is. Tell them that and give them the score, and just be yourself." True words. It's been 12 years now for me as a broadcaster, and people know my voice, and they know where the ball is. And I thank Ernie for that.

When next year comes around I'm really going to miss him.

Ernie rekindles faith in mankind

Tom Hamilton, Cleveland Indians

When I started with the Indians in 1990, the broadcasters were the people I was more in awe of than I was of the players. The broadcasters were the guys I looked to emulate, not the players. I was in awe the first time I met Bob Uecker, Jack Buck, Ernie Harwell, Vin Scully, because I thought, "I don't belong on this same platform." The real treat for me has been that all of them have been such great people, and Ernie is at the top of the list when you talk about people.

That has been the most refreshing thing for me. These people were even better people than they were broadcasters. It rekindles your faith in mankind, because you were wondering if these people were going to be stuffy or unapproachable. People like Ernie and the man I broke in with, Herb Score, made you feel like you were one of their peers.

This is kind of an end of an era. We're never going to have an era of broadcasters like this again. The business has changed, and the medium has changed. Television is much more of a factor, although baseball and radio are still a great marriage.

You talk about Hank Aaron, Willie Mays and Bob Gibson. You're also talking in the same vein about Ernie Harwell, Jack Buck, Harry Caray and Vin Scully. The likes of those people we'll never have again.

Ernie's reminders useful

Eric Nadel, Texas Rangers

I listened to Ernie for three years when I was doing minor league hockey in Muskegon. I remember most notably the joy in his voice every night when he signed on the air. It was clear he was happy to be there. It was clear he was exactly where he wanted to be at that time and loving every moment of it.

I remember as a first-year professional radio announcer noticing how descriptive he was, how well he used the language. A lot of people take short-cuts in radio, especially with the great spread of TV. And anytime I listen to Ernie, I'm reminded, "Don't take any shortcuts." You are the eyes of the audience, and nobody has ever done that as well as he does.

From when I actually got to meet him, it has been astounding to me, and I think to all of us in this business, just what a regular guy he is, how unaffected he is by all the success, how truly humble he is, and how genuinely appreciative he is every single time someone tells him that they are a listener and they enjoy his work or they've been affected by his work.

I've gone to him and asked him a lot about the use of stats. He doesn't use many. He still does it kind of the old-fashioned way. He has illuminated me on some things that he thinks are interesting and some things that he thinks are just bogging the game down with too many numbers. That's a very useful reminder to me.

This has to be a nice person
Tom Cheek, Toronto Blue Jays

When I got this opportunity when the Blue Jays came along in 1977, I got two pieces of mail. One was a note pecked out on a typewriter. It was from Ernie Harwell: "Welcome to the big leagues. I know you're going to be a big success. If there is ever anything I can do for you, here's my phone number." I thought, "Wow!" I knew little of Ernie Harwell other than, "This has to be a nice person."

In our first spring training, he lived near our training camp in Dunedin, Fla. He said, "Lulu and I would like for you and your wife to come over and have a dish of ice cream."

How often are you invited in these days and times for a dish of ice cream? That's exactly what it was, and that is Ernie Harwell. There's only one Ernie.

Ernie took me under his wing

Herb Carneal, Minnesota Twins

When I got my first full-time major league job, working with Ernie in Baltimore in 1957, my wife and I went to Baltimore to house-hunt. Ernie and his wife, Lulu, invited us to stay at their house for as long as we needed to while we were looking around for a house. And I had never met Ernie. I thought, "This is really something."

Ernie took me under his wing. In those days we did radio and television. We talked about the differences in the two, and Ernie said, "Herb, when you are doing radio, your listeners don't know anything until you tell them something." I've never forgotten that.

People ask Ernie and me why we keep doing it. It's not like a 9-to-5 job. When you come to the ballpark, you don't have any idea what's going to happen that night.

From voice on radio to colleague

Denny Matthews, K.C. Royals

When I was growing up in central Illinois, I had the pleasure of picking up lot of radio stations and a lot of different broadcasts and broadcasters, and I had the pleasure of listening to Ernie many a night.

I had the pleasure of meeting him when I got into broadcasting in 1969. I can recall how generous he was with information, how helpful he was, how encouraging he was to a young broadcaster just out of college with basically no experience.

Then I had the immense pleasure of working with Ernie on the 1982 American League championship series on CBS Radio. Just a chance to work with him, having listened to him and having known him, was unbelievable.

Ernie sparked interest in history

Ryan Lefebvre, Kansas City Royals

My first four or five years in the league, I was the youngest announcer and he was the oldest. But other than his experience and my lack of it, there was no gap between us. He treated you like a peer. I've had a lot of great discussions with him over the years about the history of broadcasting. I'm interested in what it was like in the '40s and '50s. I've really developed a sense of broadcast history because of Ernie.

Ernie is bigger than the game

Jerry Howarth, Toronto Blue Jays

Ernie has been a mentor for me. He's a wonderful Christian man whom I've emulated. He's bigger than the game because he lets the game take place and then he just calls what happens. I'm so impressed with how fundamental he is in his life and his calling of a ballgame. I saw things like discipline and routine in Ernie, and I said, "I want to do that for myself."

Ernie is a master of description

Dave Niehaus, Seattle Mariners

Ernie and Vin Scully are two of the remaining announcers who cut their teeth on radio only and had to really learn how to utilize the English language, learn how really to describe the game and make explicitly clear what was happening on the field: where the ball was, how many feet it was away from the wall, how green the grass is, were there white puffy clouds in the sky or was it a clear, cerulean blue sky. And how far the walls were from the plate down the line and in the gaps. You had to tell them. People see on television. They don't see that on radio. And Ernie is a master of describing a baseball game, as is Vin Scully.

Ernie has his own way of describing a baseball game. When you hear Ernie Harwell, you know it's Ernie Harwell. When you hear Vin Scully, nobody has to tell you who it is. You've got to develop your own style.

When an announcer has the longevity with a club that Ernie does, he becomes identified even more with the club than the stars itself. The Kalines and the icons of the game pass through here. They have exciting years like 1968, and they turn the town on. They turn the town on with their talent, and the baseball announcer turns the town on as much as he can every year with his talent, whether you win a championship or not.

People tune in to listen because it's Ernie Harwell and it's baseball. When you lose, people are still there on the other side of that radio speaker. A baseball announcer is like a member of your family.

Big shoes to fill

Rick Rizzs, Seattle Mariners

Rizzs replaced Harwell as the Tigers' lead voice in 1992, then rejoined Seattle's broadcast team when the Tigers fired him in '94.

My relationship with Ernie started when I first got to the big leagues in 1983 with the Mariners. When I came to Detroit to work for the Tigers, our relationship didn't change.

I remember all the turmoil here in 1991 with the fans knowing that was supposedly going to be Ernie's final year. He came up to me behind the batting cage at Tiger Stadium and said, "Rick, I want you to apply for my job."

I told him, "Ernie, I feel sorry for the poor son-of-a-gun who has to replace you."

He said, "No, no, Rick you can do it. You've been in the big leagues now for nine years. You've been to the minor leagues. You've got the experience. I want you to apply for my job."

Ernie stands out because of his longevity, his caring for his craft, being so good for so long from one generation to the other — and it has been three or four generations — and love for the game. You can tell that he loves the games, loves this organization, adored the fans and they adored him. He is shared adoringly by millions of fans in this area.

When you turn on the radio, it's very comforting to know that Ernie Harwell's voice is there. And I knew that in spring training in 1992 that for the first time in 33 years, fans here were going to hear a different voice than Ernie Harwell. So the first thing I made sure of was that I gave all the respect in the world and said the right things to honor Ernie Harwell.

I came back to Seattle after Detroit. Ernie and I continue to have a great deal of respect for one another.

His departure is the end of an era. This is a chapter we'll never read about again, once he's gone. It was so important that Ernie decide when he leaves. That's the way it should have been in the first place. Then there wouldn't have been so much acrimony, like there was back in 1992 when I got here. But this is Ernie's decision. It's a good one. He's been so great to baseball, not only baseball in Detroit but around the country. He's going to be missed not only by the fans here, but folks like ourselves who get to spend time with him. He's a treasure.

Ernie shared his magic

Frank Beckmann, Detroit Tigers

My favorite personal Ernie story comes from my first year of doing radio for the Tigers in 1995. Halfway through spring training, the spring with replacement players, I thought I was not doing a good job. I thought I was in a slump. I missed a couple of calls. I was really down on myself. I called Ernie, and I said, "Frankly, I feel I'm not doing a good job."

He said, "What do you mean? I think you're doing terrific."

I said, "Last night, and I know the lighting isn't good, I didn't track a ball well. I think I called it really badly."

He said, "I didn't hear that at all. I thought the broadcast sounded really good."

I said, "You're kidding?"

He said, "No, I'm serious."

I said, "Did you ever go through this?"

He said, "Frank, everybody does. What you've got to remember is that only half of the people are listening, and the other half only hear half of what you say. You're going to make mistakes. We all make them. You've got to forget them and move on."

After that, it was a piece of cake for me. I'll never forget the support he gave me as a baseball broadcaster, especially in my first year.

Ernie has never taken himself too seriously. He is offering entertainment as a baseball announcer. He's not here to solve world problems. He's helping people pass the time with baseball. That's part of what the magic of Ernie Harwell is.

Ernie gave his all to anyone

Dan Dickerson, Detroit Tigers

It was probably in the mid-'80s that I met him. We had a rotisserie baseball league in Grand Rapids. He was in town for a book signing. The head of the league invited Ernie to our end-of-the-season party, and of course Ernie being Ernie, he comes to this guy's house. That's Ernie. He's formed all these wonderful friendships on the road because fans call him out of the blue — they don't know him, he doesn't know them — and he says, "Yes, I'll go to lunch with you." And he's got these incredible friendships all over the country because he's willing to take a chance and meet people.

After I did my first Michigan football game in 1995 — when Frank Beckmann would do the Tigers through September, and they needed a sub — I got a note in the mail three days later from Ernie Harwell. It was one sentence: "I heard your first broadcast — it was terrific." I don't think I had been in touch with him for years. But that's the kind of thing he does.

We were in Baltimore this year, and my brother was there with his son. They came up to the booth for a brief visit. Ernie was throwing out the first pitch that day. My nephew, who is 10, watches Ernie do that and thinks that's kind of neat. We tell him a little about Ernie.

All my nephew wants that day is to get a ball. My brother and I are talking in the hallway outside the booth when Ernie comes up from the field after throwing out the first pitch. He sees me with my brother, whom he's met, and with my nephew. He reaches into his pocket, pulls out the ball that he's just thrown out for the first pitch in his last game in Baltimore, and gives it to my nephew, who's absolutely speechless.

Ernie's simply the best
Jim Price, Detroit Tigers

Ernie's being in a good mood every day is the most phenomenal thing I've ever seen in my life. He's like one of these young ballplayers we just brought up from Toledo: always in a good mood, always kidding. One of the guys. You can't get anything by him.

He's the best broadcaster I've ever heard because he keeps it simple. He and I think statistics are overused. The most important statistic according to Ernie is runs scored.

Index

INDEX

INDEX

Ernie Harwell is legendary for his dedication to staying fit. As a spokesman for Blue Cross/Blue Shield of Michigan, he heads up an effort in the state that urges people to walk for fitness.

About the author

Ernie Harwell was born in Washington, Ga., on Jan. 25, 1918. He began his career in radio and television in 1940 and has been broadcasting major league baseball since 1948. He retired after the 2002 Tigers season. He has written four other books – "Stories From My Life In Baseball," "Tuned To Baseball," "Diamond Gems" and "The Babe Signed My Shoe." He lives in Novi, Mich., with his wife, Lulu.